The World's Greatest Golf Courses

Bob Weeks

Foreword by Robert Trent Jones, Sr.

CRESCENT BOOKS

New York/Avenel, New Jersey

This 1992 edition published by Crescent Books,
distributed by Outlet Book Company, Inc.,
a Random House Company,
40 Engelhard Avenue
Avenel, New Jersey 07001

This book was designed and produced by
Todtri Productions Limited
P.O. Box 20058
New York, NY 10023-1482

Printed and Bound in Singapore

Library of Congress Catalog Card Number 91-73898

ISBN 0-517-06698-X
87654321

Author: Bob Weeks
Producer: Robert M. Tod
Designer and Art Director: Mark Weinberg
Editor: Mary Forsell
Typeset and Page Makeup: Strong Silent Type/NYC

TABLE OF CONTENTS

1. **Banff Springs,** *Alberta*
2. **Glen Abbey,** *Ontario*
3. **Jasper Park,** *Alberta*
4. **Kananaskis,** *Alberta*
5. **The National,** *Ontario*
6. **Augusta National,** *Georgia*
7. **Baltusrol,** *New Jersey*
8. **Colonial,** *Texas*
9. **Cypress Point,** *California*
10. **Doral,** *Florida*
11. **Firestone,** *Ohio*
12. **Harbour Town,** *South Carolina*
13. **Kiawah,** *South Carolina*
14. **Merion,** *Pennsylvania*
15. **Muirfield Village,** *Ohio*

16. **Oak Hill,** *New York*
17. **Oakland Hills,** *Michigan*
18. **Oakmont,** *Pennsylvania*
19. **Oak Tree,** *Oklahoma*
20. **The Olympic Club,** *California*
21. **Pebble Beach Golf Links,** *California*
22. **PGA West,** *California*
23. **Pinehurst No. 2,** *North Carolina*
24. **Pine Valley,** *New Jersey*
25. **Shinnecock Hills,** *New York*
26. **Spyglass Hill,** *California*
27. **Robert Trent Jones,** *Virginia*
28. **Winged Foot,** *New York*
29. **Casa de Campo,** *Dominican Republic*
30. **Dorado Beach,** *Puerto Rico*

31. **Lagunita,** *Venezuela*
32. **Mid Ocean,** *Bermuda*
33. **Tryall,** *Jamaica*
34. **Ballybunion,** *Republic of Ireland*
35. **Carnoustie,** *Scotland*
36. **Castelconturbia,** *Italy*
37. **Chantilly,** *France*
38. **Royal County Down,** *Northern Ireland*
39. **Royal Dornoch,** *Scotland*
40. **Falsterbo,** *Sweden*
41. **Muirfield,** *Scotland*
42. **Portmarnock,** *Republic of Ireland*
43. **Quinta da Marinha,** *Portugal*
44. **Royal and Ancient Golf Club of St. Andrews,** *Scotland*
45. **Sotogrande,** *Spain*

46. **Sunningdale,** *England*
47. **Royal Troon,** *Scotland*
48. **Turnberry,** *Scotland*
49. **Vilamoura,** *Portugal*
50. **Club Zur Vahr,** *Germany*
51. **Bali Handara Kosaido,** *Indonesia*
52. **Durban,** *South Africa*
53. **Fujioka Country Club,** *Japan*
54. **Royal Hong Kong,** *Hong Kong*
55. **Royal Melbourne,** *Australia*
56. **New South Wales,** *Australia*
57. **Paraparaumu Beach,** *New Zealand*
58. **Shinyo Country Club,** *Japan*
59. **Titirangi,** *New Zealand*
60. **Wairakei,** *New Zealand*

The 18th
at Muirfield,
Scotland.

I N T R O D U C T I O N

In my travels, it never ceases to amaze me the very few places in this world where golf courses do *not* exist. Whether it is a par-three municipal course where the hopes and dreams of many young players are nurtured; a course located in a remote, Third World area that acts not only as a place to golf but as a home for refugees; or one of the exotic new real estate courses springing up throughout the Western world, it is hard to find a place where one cannot get a fix for his or her golf obsession.

From Yellowknife in Canada's Arctic to the tip of New Zealand's South Island, from the beautiful Monterey peninsula in America to the Scottish links, on every continent, in hundreds of countries, golf is played. Yet in all these places, no two courses are the same. Each is unique and each has something to offer players of this fastest-growing game.

Perhaps that is what makes golf so grand—because, unlike any other sport, the playing field in golf is never the same. And what pleases one player is another's frustration. Fast greens, slow greens, par threes, par fives, uphill, downhill—the combinations and design possibilities are endless. In this book, we present sixty wonderful courses from around the world. I hope when you read about them, memories will return or dreams will be born.

—Bob Weeks

F O R E W O R D

Traveling the world as I have for the greater part of sixty years, laying out a length of fairways that might encircle the globe, has afforded me a continuing opportunity to view, appraise, and absorb the features and character of some of the world's finest golf courses and to realize why they are great.

Although all have one thing in common as venues for playing the greatest game ever conceived for the pleasure of man, each is distinct for the way it was deployed as a challenge,the setting and terrain on which it is situated, and the singular and, ofttimes, peculiar charm with which it has been endowed to set it apart from all the rest.

The selections in this book, a majority of which I have included in my memory bank under the index of "greatness," would be worthy as sites for any championship currently on the worldwide schedule. They are an outstanding collection, and for golfers who never will trod their fairways, the details and descriptions of them will afford the next best insights into why they warrant inclusion in this collection.

The author has been most complimentary to me and to my work, as he has included a half dozen courses of my doing, including the new Robert Trent Jones Golf Club on Lake Manassas, Virginia, in addition to a like number of courses that it was my pleasure to rework and remodel for national championships, such as Baltusrol Golf Club, Firestone Country Club, Oakland Hills Country Club and, to a lesser degree, the Olympic Club, Oakmont Country Club, and Augusta National Golf Club.

THE WORLD'S GREATEST GOLF COURSES is just that—and as one who has spent a lifetime in the game, the most sincere comment I can make is that the next best thing to playing them is to read this book.
—Robert Trent Jones

e 11th at
bert Trent
nes Intl.
lf Club.

The Americas and Caribbean

Kiawah's 18th hole sits quietly in the dunes waiting to challenge golfers.

Banff Springs *Banff, Alberta*

The mountains combine with huge fir trees to create an incredible sight. Banff Springs is as beautiful as it is challenging.

Carved out of the majestic Rockies, the Banff Springs Golf Course is as beautiful as it is demanding. With towering peaks, glacial lakes, and an outstanding design, the course has all the ingredients for great golf.

Banff Springs was built in 1927 by Canadian architect Stanley Thompson and carries the dubious distinction of being the first course to cost more than $1 million to complete. By the looks of things, however, it would appear the Canadian Pacific Railway, which commissioned the work, received value for its investment.

The original eighteen holes required plenty of rock blasting and earth moving, and the creation of the course with the tools available at that time is a story in itself. These two nines, known as Rundle and Sulphur, were joined in 1989 by another nine holes, Tunnel, which only enhances the pleasure of the course.

The par-three holes at Banff Springs are all memorable. The famed Devil's Cauldron is one of the most photographed holes in the world. An elevated tee sits above a glacial lake that offers protection for a sloping green 170 yards away. The combination of the mountain elevation and gusting winds makes club selection a difficult task.

Anywhere on the course the jutting mountains add a breathtakingly gorgeous, distinctive backdrop. Each hole seems to bring a new perspective more beautiful than the previous one.

From many places on the course, the impressive-looking Banff Springs hotel can be seen in the distance, offering perhaps a bit of encouragement to players who are near completion of their round and know they can soon retire to the luxury and pampering of the century-old resort.

Banff Springs was the first golf course to cost more than $1 million to construct.

The Majestic Banff Springs Hotel serves as a beacon for weary golfers.

Glen Abbey
Oakville, Ontario

Few countries have a permanent site for their national championships, but then few countries have a course like Glen Abbey, home of the Canadian Open championship. Glen Abbey is a tournament-tough course that has many moods. One day, it can play long and tough, while on another, it can be tamed by even the shortest of hitters. But it is safe to say when the world's best come to the Abbey each year for the Canadian championship, the course always provides a challenge.

Glen Abbey was built in 1977 by Jack Nicklaus. It was the first course that Nicklaus designed by himself and, in many ways, it is still one of his best. Nicklaus has said that at Glen Abbey, he corrected many of the mistakes he made at Muirfield Village, his Ohio course.

As a tournament course, the Abbey works very well. The clubhouse is at the center of all the excitement, and various hubs work out of this central area. For spectators, that means it is very easy to see a lot of action without having to walk too far.

The course is owned by the Royal Canadian Golf Association, which purchased it in 1981, and is open to the public except when the Open is being contested. Each year, more than 30,000 rounds are played at the Abbey, with many coming from people who wish to see how they'd do on the course that has boasted such winners as Greg Norman, Curtis Strange, and Lee Trevino.

As these great players can attest, the strength of Glen Abbey is found on holes 11 through 15—known as the Valley Holes. It would be fair to say that this is where the Canadian Open is won. The descent into the valley comes on the tee shot at 11, a difficult par four that asks players to cross 16 Mile Creek with the approach shot. Players must cross this creek five more times in the next three holes before hitting the 15th, a short but difficult par three that leads them out of the valley and into three good finishing holes.

Since 1977, Glen Abbey has hosted every Canadian Open, the fourth oldest national championship in the world, with the exception of one. (In 1980 Royal Montreal was the site.) It has become a well-respected site, worthy of deciding Canada's annual golfing champion.

Jasper Park *Jasper, Alberta*

There is and always has been a happy rivalry between Jasper and Banff, the two fine Canadian mountain resorts. Much of that competition stems from the two fine golf courses at each spot.

Like Banff, Jasper sits in the Rocky Mountains and was designed by Stanley Thompson for the Canadian National Railways (CNR). However, Jasper is older than its southern neighbor by two years and despite its location, is not that similar a golf course.

Carved from the Rocky Mountains, Jasper features exceptional panoramas on every hole.

Jasper Park, ctd.

Jasper is punctuated by tree-lined fairways; this often requires pitching back to the fairway after an errant drive. Bountiful bunkering and open greens are also found throughout the course, providing a good test of approach shots.

During construction of Jasper, Thompson, noted for a devilish touch of humor, molded the 231-yard, par-three 9th so that when viewed from the tee, the curvaceous body of a woman appeared. Thompson apparently named the hole Cleopatra, and only after some gentle persuasion from the CNR did he smooth out the design.

At less than 6,600 yards, Jasper is not a long course, but it is quite challenging for golfers of any handicap. There are five par-three holes, which bring the overall par to 71, and all of them are a treat to attempt to par. Only one par-five is monstrously long, that being the 603-yard 13th hole. But in the thin mountain air, even that hole is very playable.

As a golf destination, Jasper has received much recognition and many rewards. The historic lodge is a sight to behold with huge wooden beams and rustic decor throughout. The traditions of the grand railway hotels of the turn of the century are very much alive at Jasper.

Jasper is one of a number of courses built by the Canadian railways in the 1920s and 1930s. It has remained a popular vacation destination since opening.

Jasper's beauty does not come only from the surrounding mountains. Wood and water make up a great deal of the scenery.

Kananaskis

Kananaskis Village,
Alberta

Architect Robert Trent Jones called the Kananaskis site the best he'd ever seen for a golf course.

To the list of fine Canadian mountain golf courses such as Banff Springs and Jasper Park, another name now can be safely added: Kananaskis.

The two courses that make up Kananaskis sit in the foothills of the Rocky Mountains, a half hour from Calgary. Designed by Robert Trent Jones, the project was undertaken by the provincial government of Alberta back in the early 1980s. Despite the lengthy list of Jones's work, he felt strongly enough about the area to call Kananaskis the finest location he'd ever seen for a golf course. The first of the two courses to open was Mount Lorette, a 7,100-yard layout that began play in 1983. It was followed a year later by the 7,049-yard Mount Kidd. For public courses, the length may appear intimidating. Holes such as the 615-yard second and 642-yard 18th at Mount Kidd seem out of reach for the longest of ball strikers, but the elevation and mountain air provide for some advantageous distance on hits that will bring the courses back to mid-handicap standards.

Despite being close to the mountains, Kananaskis is a relatively flat golf course. Water is more of a hazard than hills.

Despite the surrounding mountains, both Kananaskis courses are relatively flat, but water and sand are plentiful and make placement a premium on both courses. Greens are always fair and not particularly deceiving. What you see is usually what you get.

It is easy for a golfer to lose his or her concentration in the mountain splendor at Kananaskis. The wooded beauty leading to the snow-peaked mountains is a visual treat unlike any other in golf. Regardless of your score, a round at either Kananaskis course is time well spent.

ing golfers the long and narrow par-five 4th. As with so many of the holes at the National, placement off the tee is essential on the 4th hole, which features a slim landing area. The second shot crosses a creek, while the third is usually played with a short iron or wedge into a well-bunkered, elevated green. The 4th hole, certainly one of the most demanding on the course, will set the tone for what is to come.

The 4th hole at The National, a long par five with a meandering stream running through it, is typical of the difficult beauty at Canada's top-ranked course.

The National *Woodbridge, Ontario*

Despite its relative youth, the National Golf Club is perennially rated as the top course in Canada. After playing a round here, it's easy to understand why it continues to receive such accolades.

The National, designed by Tom and George Fazio, opened for play in 1974. The course was built by Toronto businessman Gil Blechman, who challenged the Fazios to build a layout on which the U.S. Open could be played in twenty-four hours notice. While many feel he may not quite have reached that lofty goal, he did create an exciting and often breathtaking golf course. It is often hard to believe it was built in less than one year. When one considers the short Canadian growing season and long winters, this accomplishment is put into proper perspective.

The course begins with a trio of relatively straightforward holes before offer-

While there are many signature holes at the National, the most memorable stretch comes at the turn. The 10th tee to the 13th green comprise the heart of the course, and making it through this expanse in par or better must be considered a triumph.

As with so many great golf courses, the finishing holes

The 17th hole, a 42? yard par four, make? up one half of a strong finish. Wate? guards the right of the hole, while out bounds lines the entire left side.

at the National are impressive and opportune. The par-four 17th, a 428-yard hole, will allow a birdie now and then, while the 18th, an uphill, 455-yard par five, can also be beaten. With exceptional grooming, eye-catching scenery, and solid golf holes, the National is a treat to play.

A round at the National is usually decided by a series of three holes, which begins here at the 11th. The par four features a deceptive green, which is farther than it looks.

Augusta National
Augusta, Georgia

In all of the United States, there is probably no more hallowed golfing ground than the Augusta National Golf Club. The mere mention of the name conjures up many memories that have become legend in golf history. The Sarazan double eagle, de Vicenzo's incorrect scorecard, Mize's chip, the return of Nicklaus in '86. Great moments that all had one common element: Augusta.

It comes as no surprise to anyone that the distinguished course has equally distinguished roots. Its founder was Bobby Jones, perhaps the best amateur golfer of all time. Jones created the course with help of Alister Mackenzie, the architect of Cypress Point in California, but it was Jones's touch and influence that directed the design.

Working with piece of land that had formerly been a nursery, Jones and Mackenzie came up with a spectacular layout that is strong enough to test the best players in the world each year at the Masters, yet subtle enough that midhandicap members can enjoy its grace.

Perhaps the only change from the original course unveiled in 1933 was the changing of the nines. Jones reversed them in 1935 because he felt the 9th was a stronger finishing hole. Today, while small alterations have been made, the course is true to its origins.

Augusta National was constructed by Bobby Jones and Alister Mackenzie on land that was once home to a nursery.

The 13th is the final hole in the trio known as Amen Corner, where the Masters has been decided on so many occasions.

While recognized for its difficulty, Augusta National is also an exceedingly beautiful golf course, as the 12th hole can attest.

Every step of the way has Bobby Jones's name on it.

There is nothing hard-edged about Augusta. The fairways roll gently and greens slope delicately in many directions. The course flows from hole to hole with a seamless appearance. Nothing is done in extreme at Augusta, either—consider that there are only forty-six bunkers, yet everyone can affect play.

Many of the holes at Augusta National are as well known to television viewers as they are to the Augusta members, even though most of the former have never set foot on the course. The 11th, 12th, and 13th, which make up Amen Corner, have more often than not been the deciding factors in the Masters. And 16, the long par three over the water, which often teases players with the pin position; 17, the challenging par four; and 18, the distinctive home hole, give the course an excellent finish.

Like its founder, Augusta National has provided so many cherished moments to the game that it will always have a special place in the history of golf.

Pin placements on the par-three 16th can run from easy to down-right nasty.

Baltusrol (Lower Course)

Springfield, New Jersey

The Lower Course at the Baltusrol Golf Club is perhaps best known for two holes: the par-three 4th and the par-five 17th. Both are among the most daring in golf. The two have been the deciding factors in U.S. Open championships as well as $2 nassau games among members.

But the remaining sixteen holes at Baltusrol are equally challenging, making the course one of the finest in the United States. Baltusrol is named after Baltus Roll, a farmer who owned the land upon which the course is built. The Lower Course was designed by A.W. Tillinghast, a somewhat eccentric architect who is given credit for coming up with the term "birdie" for a score of one under par on a hole. One of the most unusual architectural features of Baltusrol is that the final two holes are both par fives. Another odd fact is that the course is one of few anywhere that has been shortened for professional tournaments. That fact is somewhat misleading as the par is

changed from 72 to 70 with the 1st hole—a par five—being shortened to become a par four.

In 1954, the course was remodeled by Robert Trent Jones in preparation for the 1954 U.S. Open. It was Jones who touched up the 4th hole into one of the great par threes in American golf. Playing anywhere from 155 to 195 yards, depending on the tee position, the initial shot must carry an imposing pond that protects every inch of the hole leading up to the green. Clear the pond and you're on the green. If you're not on the green, you're usually wet.

The 17th hole has been praised as one of golf's best par fives by many, including Jack Nicklaus. At 630 yards, it is the longest hole ever played in the U.S. Open. In addition to its monumental length, the 17th has more sand than the average desert. About halfway down the hole, a stretch of the hazard known, appropriately, as the Sahara crosses the fairway, which adds to the challenge.

Baltusrol has been the site of thirteen U.S. national championships, including Jack Nicklaus's victory in the 1980 U.S. Open. It is a fitting course upon which to decide the country's best.

The 4th is one of the great par-three holes in the United States. Robert Trent Jones reworked it into its present state in preparation for the 1954 U.S. Open.

The Lower course ends with back-to-back par fives, a rarity among championship courses. The 18th is a dramatic conclusion to a round at this New Jersey club.

Colonial *Fort Worth, Texas*

The Colonial Country Club was designed by one of the most unusual golf course architects ever to ply his trade. John Bredemus, who built the Fort Worth club in 1935, was known for such unusual characteristics as his hatred of shoes, his refusal to use new golf balls, and his penchant for planning courses while perched in tall trees. While he may have been somewhat odd, his design at Colonial is brilliant and has been largely unchanged over the years.

Colonial was masterminded by Texas department store owner Marvin Leonard, who dreamed of a course where a U.S. Open could be held. Leonard was also one of the backers of a young Ben Hogan; the latter became synonymous with Colonial.

In 1941, Leonard got his wish, as the U.S. Open came to Colonial. Craig Wood won the title with a four-over-par score of 284, which he accomplished while wear-

ing a brace to help an ailing back. More recently, the 1991 U.S. Women's Open was held at Colonial, with Meg Mallon earning the victory.

While national championships have been contested at the Texas course, the Colonial Invitational, a regular stop on the PGA Tour, has given the course its outstanding reputation.

Each year, the tour's top players learn the subtle difficulties of the course in one of the year's top events. Perhaps most fitting is that Ben Hogan has taken the championship in that event five times. Many have said that he could play the course better than anyone and that his exceptional talents were partly a result of playing Colonial so often. If he could master this course, any other would be a cinch.

A wall of champions sits proudly at Colonial, recording the names of those who have captured the invitational tournament. It is filled with great names, but none are loved more at the course than Hogan. Hogan was known for his precision—and that is the most desired commodity of a round at Colonial. The course can play to just over 7,000 yards, but the great difficulty is positioning the ball off the tee to set up second shots. Delicate doglegs lined by trees of pecan and oak are everywhere and force some course management out of

every golfer.

The greens are small and tough to read. Many breaks that don't seem there suddenly appear, usually after the golfer has stroked the ball. Patience is definitely needed when putting.

Colonial is a distinguished course that is tough but fair. It is not tricked up in any way, and golfers of all abilities respect that. It has a glorious past and should continue in its revered stature for some time to come.

Ben Hogan played his early golf at Colonial, which many observers say led in part to his great success.
The Colonial Invitational, one of the top PGA Tour events, is held annually at the Fort Worth course.

At 466 yards, the 5th hole requires a long drive with a left-to-right draw for a reasonable chance of hitting the green in regulation.

Cypress Point

Pebble Beach, California

Perhaps the most amazing thing about Cypress Point is that it defies all the usual criteria for a great golf course. First, it is not a long course, stretching only a little more than 6,500 yards. Second, it has a strange routing with back-to-back par threes and par fives. But the exceptional land upon which the course is built makes up for any unconventional features. Cypress Point is considered by many to be the most beautiful golf course in the world. It would be hard to make a strong argument against that assessment.

It is not uncommon to hit a driver from the tee on 16. The carry to the green is more than 200 yards.

Cypress Point was opened in 1928 after a design by Alister Mackenzie. It was his work at this course that led Bobby Jones to ask Mackenzie to work with him at Augusta National.

The course is tucked into the end of the Monterey Peninsula on land that juts out into the Pacific Ocean with a craggy rockface surrounding the shore. The ocean can batter the course when it is angry and provide a serene backdrop on calmer days. No matter what the weather, though, the ocean contributes greatly to the course's beauty.

If Cypress Point is known for anything, it is a trio of holes that caress the shore: the 15th, 16th, and 17th. At 139 yards, the 15th is the shortest hole on the course, and a wedge or nine iron will usually be enough club. The shot is played across a steep crevice with the pounding surf providing a suitable distraction.

The 16th is another par three but much longer. At 233 yards, this hole will often require a driver if the wind is up. The tee shot is played over an ocean inlet with a carry

Among the most beautiful golf holes in the world is the 15th at Cypress Point, the shortest hole on the course.

Cypress Point, Ctd.

of more than 200 yards needed to reach the green. This may be one of the most difficult shots in golf. (For the timid, however, there is a bail-out area to the left.)

Before catching your breath after the 16th, the 17th hole awaits. A dogleg right, the hole is just under 400 yards long. From the tee, players must drive the ball over another section of the rocky cliffs to a fairway that demands precision. The important factor is not to be blocked out by a large pine that hides the right side of the fairway and comes into play on the second shot. A four here will be well earned.

Despite not conforming to standards usually laid out for golf courses, few people would doubt the inclusion of Cypress Point among the world's best.

Despite not sharing any of the criteria good golf courses have in common, Cypress Point is as tough as it is pretty.

Tucked into the sand, the 9th hole sits like an oasis among the scrub.

Doral

Miami, Florida

With a nickname of the Monster, it's hard not to be intimidated by the Blue course at the Doral Country Club. In reality, it is an imaginative and exciting course that will test golfers of all handicaps.

As with most golf courses in Florida, Doral is built largely on flat land. In 1962, prior to the city's boom period, real estate developer Alfred Kaskel bought a large parcel of land near the Miami airport. Architect Dick Wilson took the swampy acreage and designed a layout that has inspired players for many years.

There are eight lakes with which to contend at Doral and very few holes don't have some type of watery hazard. At just less than 7,000 yards, most players will need some distance off the tee, which pre-sents a bit of a quandary: being accurate to avoid the water is necessary, but so is hitting it long enough to reach the green in regulation. On several holes, decisions must be made of whether to sacrifice accuracy or distance.

The 8th hole at Doral is a dramatic par five of 528 yards that calls for two shots, the second and third, to be played across water. The green is set out into one of the lakes, leaving little margin for error with the approach shot. Anything less than perfect will result in a wet ball. A par is usually a satisfying result for this hole.

The most famous of holes at Doral is the 18th, a 425-yard par four, known as the Blue Monster. Water is found down the entire left side of the hole, and the prevailing wind usually helps draw the ball waterward. This means there is great demand for an accurate tee shot. Even with a solid hit off the tee, a long iron is the norm for the second shot into a green that is protected by water in front and bunkers behind.

During the PGA Tour's annual pilgrimage to the course for the Doral Open, the best players in the world are usually humbled by the 18th. It often ranks as the toughest finishing hole of the year on the tour.

Doral is more than just the Blue course. There are actually six layouts in total, one of

The 18th, the Blue Monster, has taken its toll on professionals and amateurs alike.

32

which is a nine-hole track. The accompanying resort is among the most luxurious in the United States and attracts large numbers of golfing visitors annually. Close to 90 percent of all rounds at Doral's courses are played by guests.

The 13th hole at the Blue course. There are five championship golf courses at Doral, making it one of the world's largest golf resorts.

Very few golf courses at Doral don't have some kind water hazard. Architect Dick Wilson transformed swampy land near the Miami airport into Doral.

Firestone

Akron, Ohio

Firestone was started as an incentive for employees at the huge tire and rubber company.

The 16th hole is one of the most difficult holes on the golf course. The pond in front of the green and its length of 625 yards virtually prohibits going for it in two

An event with such an impressive name as the World Series of Golf would certainly call for a course of world-class proportions as its site. And since the inception of the tournament, the host course has been the Firestone Country Club. To all competitors and spectators, this course certainly meets all the necessary criteria. It is a long and treacherous course that needs both strength and finesse to tackle.

The Firestone layout was initiated by Harvey Firestone Sr., founder of the giant tire and rubber company, as an incentive to his employees. Designed by Bertie Way, runner-up in the 1899 U.S. Open, the course (now known as the South Course) opened in 1929 and was popular if not all that difficult.

In the 1950s, with professional golf on the rise, Firestone saw that forming an alliance with the high-profile players would be a good way to promote the company's products. At that time, it began an association with the Rubber City Open, a popular tour event, that was to last until 1959.

With that sponsorship commitment firmly established, the Firestone course was invited to host the 1960 PGA Championship. After accepting, the course was given over to the hand of Robert Trent Jones for alterations worthy of a major championship.

Trent Jones, however, did more than just a touch-up on the Firestone course. Drastic changes included adding some 600 yards to its length, putting in more than fifty bunkers, remodeling sixteen greens, and building two completely new ones, as well as adding two ponds. Many have called it Trent Jones's best work.

At 7,150 yards and a par of 70, Firestone is excruciatingly long. A perfect example of this is the 16th, a par five of 625 yards. Although the hole plays entirely downhill, it is still somewhat of a monster to tame. To add to the difficulty, a pond is found in front of the green making it nearly impossible to reach the putting surface in two shots.

The 18th is one of golf's famous finishing holes, thanks in large part to the many televised events played at Firestone. A 465-yard par four, it starts at an elevated tee and moves on to a fairway that has a thick stand of trees on the left side. Second shots are played with a long iron or wood to a heavily bunkered green.

The entire Firestone course is like the 18th. Players here will certainly give their long irons a workout. Being straight with them is an absolute must.

Today, Firestone is known as the home of the World Series of Golf, an annual meeting of the globe's best players that began in 1962 when Walter Schwimmer, a Chicago producer, put up a $50,000 prize. It is one of the top stops on the PGA Tour each year, drawing a large international corps of golfers, many of whom are humbled by Firestone.

The green on the long, par-three 7th hole is guarded by numerous bunkers.

Harbour Town

*Hilton Head Island,
South Carolina*

With Calibogue Sound running down the entire left side and the candy-striped lighthouse at the end, the 18th hole is one of the best finishes in golf.

Built by Pete Dye with help from Jack Nicklaus, Harbour Town hosted the PGA Tour's Heritage Classic just after opening.

If Pete Dye is known for one course out of all of his fine designs, it would have to be Harbour Town. It may not be his best work, or even the most difficult course he has constructed, but Harbour Town is what golf is all about. It's calm and serene with just enough bite to make it a difficult test for the world's best golfers. It doesn't have many hard edges or brash signature holes. Instead, the course flows smoothly—the sum of its parts that makes Harbour Town what it is.

Dye designed Harbour Town along with consultant Jack Nicklaus in 1969 on the resort of Hilton Head Island. Just a few months after it opened, the course hosted the Heritage Classic, a tour event that was won by Arnold Palmer. That tournament has become an annual event at Harbour Town with such names as Johnny Miller, Hale Irwin, Jack Nicklaus, Greg Norman, and Nick Faldo emerging victorious.

From the back tees, Harbour Town reaches only 6,912 yards, not particularly long by professional standards. It is built on mostly flat land, and the holes seldom rise or fall with any severity. At first glance, it may not seem that tough at all. However, the fairways offer a great deal of the difficulty; they have a narrow appearance thanks to the many oaks, pines, and magnolias framing them. This puts a premium on tee shots. It is of the utmost importance that the first shot on every hole at Harbour Town be carefully considered before being hit. Going off line just slightly can mean a quick bogey. More complications come at the greens at Harbour Town, which are quite small and deceptive in their undulations.

Harbour Town's 18th hole provides one of the classic finishes in American golf. With the Calibogue Sound running down the entire left side of the hole, two shots must carry water before reaching the green in regulation. The par-four hole, which can play as long as 478 yards, is dominated by the famous candy-striped lighthouse, which appears behind the green and acts as a beacon for golf balls as well as ships. Many exciting moments have occurred at this hole, with the great list of Heritage champions conquering it to claim the title. The great finish is only fitting on such a great golf course.

Like many holes, the 16th features narrow fairways and relatively small greens.

37

Kiawah Island
(Ocean Course)
*Kiawah Island,
South Carolina*

**Created by Pete
Dye, the Ocean
Course rests in
a strip of sandy
land beside the
Atlantic Ocean.**

Natural is hardly a word associated with many of architect Pete Dye's works, but the Ocean Course could be called very little else. The site of the 1991 Ryder Cup Matches, the Ocean Course is quite reminiscent of Scottish courses, with dunes, grasses, and winds forming and reforming the land. Here is a course that doesn't seem to have been created as much as it was found.

Built onto a thin stretch of dunes tucked beside the Atlantic Ocean, the Ocean Course at Kiawah Island is a course Dye feels may become his hallmark. So enthused about the piece of land he was given to work with, Dye actually moved to the site to be closer to his task.

The Ocean Course is as picturesque a course as any on the Eastern seaboard, with every hole offering an ocean view. But despite its beauty, this is not a walk in the park. At 7,300 yards, it is tough to tame. Dye designed many of the par-four holes with the intent of bringing the long iron back into play. With three par fours on the front nine over 450 yards from the championship tees, that goal seems to have been reached.

Even the par threes may require two and three irons, with the two shortest playing 197 yards.

While the course can play tough for tournaments, varied tee positions allow even novice amateurs a realistic chance. From the forward tee positions, the course plays to a reasonable 5,300 yards.

There are certainly some manmade features on the Ocean Course, but for the most part, its lines are smooth and even. There are no extremes here, only a continuous flow. It's a course that in only a short period of time has become an American classic.

**Kiawah was built
to host the 1991
Ryder Cup, where
holes such as the
7th played a large
part in deciding
the winner of the
biennial matches.**

**The 3rd hole
looks enchanting,
but with the
ocean breezes at
play can be diffi-
cult to par.**

Merion
(East Course)

Ardmore,

Pennsylvania

Despite being only 6,500 yards, Merion Golf Club would have to be rated as one of the greatest championship courses in America. Few other clubs can boast such a distinguished history in hosting tournaments and as respected a list of past champions. Merion always seems to bring out the best in the best players.

Founded in the late 1890s, the Merion Cricket Club, as it was known for many years, sent a young member, Hugh Wilson, on a six-month trip to Britain to study golf course architecture. Wilson returned full of ideas and energy and soon began designing a new course for the membership.

It would seem that the club's investment in its young member paid off. Although he had never built a course prior to his work at Merion, Wilson crafted an exacting lay-

The greens at Merion, such as this one on the 17th, are usually brought to extremely quick speeds during tournaments.

out using many influences— but no direct imitations—from his British trip. Completed in 1912, Wilson's course continued to be fine-tuned until his death in 1925. The challenge of Merion comes not from its length—it is the shortest course since World War II to host the U.S. Open—but in the demand placed on precision off the tees and into the greens. The fairways are not so much narrow as they are controlled. The tee shot must be placed strategically in hopes of providing a better approach to the small, hard greens of Merion.

Merion's record as a tournament site is impressive. Its first championship was the 1904 Women's Amateur, played on a forerunner to the Wilson course. A 14-year-old Bobby Jones made his U.S. Amateur debut in the 1916 championship, lasting until the quarter-finals. He returned to Merion in 1922 to capture his first Amateur

title and then completed his famous Grand Slam there with another Amateur win in 1930.

In 1950, Ben Hogan fought off severe pain in his legs to finish the Open with a score of 287. That put him in a tie with George Fazio and Lloyd Mangrum, both of whom he defeated the next day in a playoff.

In the 1971 Open, Lee Trevino and Jack Nicklaus tied at 280, quite a high score for those days. Trevino won the title the next day in another playoff and went on to win the British and Canadian Opens in the next two weeks—a record three national titles in three weeks.

Merion has always refused to yield to the best players in the game. Some think it is because of the slick greens,

often brought down to excruciatingly slippery speeds during tournaments. Walter Hagen is reported to have putted a ball off a green and out of bounds in one event played at the course, while Bobby Jones is said to have hit a putt into a creek during the 1914 Amateur.

The putting surfaces are accompanied by thick, matted rough at tournament time, making it all that much more important to hit the green in regulation. Chipping back to the hole is akin to the death penalty for the golf ball.

In total, because of the great course and fine tournament record, Merion has one of the most distinguished histories in American golf.

The 11th hole at Merion, which is the shortest course to host the U.S. Open since the Second World War.

Muirfield Village
Dublin, Ohio

The 17th hole rarely plays easy. The demanding green features subtle breaks and must be treated with care.

Few courses have been as closely tied to their designers as Muirfield Village Golf Club. Of course, when Jack Nicklaus is the person who did the designing, it easy to understand why.

In actuality, Nicklaus was only one half of the design team at Muirfield. He shared the job of laying out this grand course with Desmond Muirhead. But like Bobby Jones and Augusta, it is safe to say Muirfield Village will always be regarded as the course that Jack built.

Nicklaus put into Muirfield Village the elements of what he believed make a great golf course. He digested his likes and dislikes from the hundreds of courses he had played and molded them into his concept. He even named it after the Scottish course upon which he played his first international matches in the Walker Cup and won his first British Open in 1966.

Like its creator, Muirfield Village is nothing short of outstanding. It offers a full-bodied test of golf that can be as challenging for a professional as it is for a 20 handicapper. That,

Muirfield will always be regarded as a Jack Nicklaus course, although he collaborated with Desmond Muirhead on the job.

Muirfield, ctd.

in essence, is what defines a great golf course, and Muirfield certainly fits that bill.

The course begins calmly enough with a 446-yard par four that is a fair yet tough opening hole. But it soon rises up with holes such as the difficult par-four third of 392 yards, where the second shot is played over a pond that guards the green. At five, a creek travels down most of the left side of the 531-yard par five and also offers protection for a good portion of the green.

After the turn, the 10th hole immediately presents a difficult task. It is a 441-yard par four that demands a solid drive. On the left side of the fairway is a tree that serves as a safeguard to anyone thinking about taking the short-cut to the green.

Muirfield Village ends with a particularly tough hole, a par-four, 437-yard gem. Tournaments are won and lost here with the hole allowing fewer birdies than bogeys. Tournaments have been a large part of Muirfield Village, with Nicklaus hosting the annual Memorial event. The tournament not only draws an excellent field of the world's best players, but takes time to honor those who have given something back to the game of golf with a number of annual awards.

A good drive is a must on the tough 10th hole, a 441-yard par four.

Muirfield's finishing hole is a 437-yard par four dotted with bunkers.

Oak Hill

Rochester, New York

A long iron is the normal club used to approach the 17th hole, which has a narrow opening between two bunkers.

The 16th green rises above the fairway, and players must avoid overhanging trees with their incoming shots.

Two of the greatest architects in golf can share credit for making Oak Hill a truly classic layout. Initially, the East course was laid out by Donald Ross in 1924. In 1956 and again in 1967, Robert Trent Jones added more touches to Oak Hill, retaining the original character while adding more modern difficulty.

But it may have been an Oak Hill member, Dr. John R. Williams, who gets the most credit for building the atmosphere that surrounds the club. Williams headed a team that planted thousands of trees on the property, most of which now have grown to large proportions. These trees are the most distinguishing feature of any round at Oak Hill.

Oak Hill has been the site of many top tournaments, including U.S. Opens in 1956 (won by Cary Middlecoff), 1968 (won by Lee Trevino), and 1989 (won by Curtis Strange) and the 1980 PGA Championship (won by Jack Nicklaus). This list of winners says quite a deal about the excellence of the course.

What makes Oak Hill a tremendous tournament site is no doubt the finishing holes. Few courses can match Oak Hill for its ending, which has provided many dramatic moments to golf's history. The final trio of holes is comprised of two tough par fours and one par five, which is made into a par four during tournaments.

The 16th is a 439-yard par four with a fairway that slopes left. Thick trees line both sides of the hole, and anyone straying into them will be penalized at least one shot. An out-of-bounds area also lurks not far away on the left side. The green is protected by a bunker in front and on the right, and overhanging trees also add to the difficulty.

The 17th is 458 yards, with a bend from left to right, and the ideal drive will have a slight fade. The trees on the right are emblazoned with marks made by the balls of those players trying to cut the corner too tightly. The approach shot, usually made with a long iron, must negotiate a narrow opening to the green framed on both sides by bunkers. Putting on the 17th is not easy, as Ben Hogan can readily attest. He missed a four-foot par putt here that virtually ended his hopes of winning the '56 Open.

The 18th is a 440-yard masterpiece with a huge gulch in front of the green that will accept any ball that is less than perfect. It is a fitting end to a wonderful golf course and has been the spot on which many champions have been crowned.

Oak Hill's East course features thousands of trees planted in the course's early days. Today, they serve as narrow margins to most fairways.

Oakland Hills *Birmingham, Michigan*

Few American courses have as distinguished a tournament history as Oakland Hills Country Club. It has hosted numerous championships, including five U.S. Opens, and each one has been a thrilling tournament.

But Oakland Hills is much more than just a tournament site. It is a classic golf course that winds its way through rolling woodland. It is also a course that has grown with time and improved with age.

The course, designed by Donald Ross, was opened in 1918, with Walter Hagen serving as the first professional. It welcomed its first U.S. Open in 1927, when dark horse Cyril Walker emerged victorious. In 1937, Ralph Guldahl took home the top prize.

In 1951, the U.S. Open again came to Oakland Hills,

but not before Robert Trent Jones did a major remodeling job, adding bunkers in the fairways and beside the greens. The result was well received, with eventual winner Ben Hogan playing an incredible final 18 to overtake Bobby Locke for the title on the face-lifted layout.

Hogan, like so many members, learned the secret of scoring well at Oakland Hills is to keep the ball in the fairway. On the majority of the holes, driving to precise points is imperative and knowing when to keep the driver in the bag is equally important. While the course has been tempered somewhat in its severity since that 1951 Open, this advice remains the key to a good round.

The greens at this suburban Detroit club are also not easy to contend with; many are quite severe with slopes and grades. On the 18th, for example, it is possible to putt with your back to the hole in order to get it close.

The U.S. Open returned to Oakland Hills in 1961, when Gene Littler won, and 1985, where Andy North came out of a pack to claim the title. Gary Player also tamed the course in 1972 to take home top prize in the PGA Championship. His nine-iron shot on the 16th hole over a willow and a lake to within a few feet of the pin was the decisive shot in this event.

With a great tournament history, it is hard not to feel the ghosts of past champions when playing at Oakland Hills. Their presence, as well as that of a great golf course, make golf here more than a game.

On greens such as the 18th, the slopes are severe enough to frustrate the most accomplished of putters.

Oakland Hill's 10th hole starts the back nine off in dramatic fashion.

The par-three 17th is an uphill hole with a challenging green.

Oakmont

Oakmont, Pennsylvania

The Church Pew bunkers are an interesting hazard to look at, but a difficult one from which to extract a ball.

Mention the name Oakmont to touring professionals and you detect a look of terror enter their eyes. For even the best golfers in the world are in awe of this course, located in the foothills of the Alleghenies. It is as difficult and intense a course as there is in North America, maybe the world.

Oakmont, which opened in 1904, was the personal project of steel magnate Henry C. Fownes. His son, William—the Amateur champion in 1910 and United States Golf Association president in 1926 and 1927—then cultivated the course in its early years. When the course first opened, it had five par fives and a par six, as well as more than two hundred bunkers. It was said that Henry Fownes continually added new bunkers each time he learned the existing ones had been carried by a long hitter.

While more than thirty bunkers have been removed from the course, there is still enough sand at Oakmont to build a small beach. The bunkers are of every shape and style. The most challenging comes at the 3rd and 4th holes: the famous Church Pews, where a bunker in excess of 100 yards in length is broken up by long, symmetrical strips of grass.

So fond was Fownes of his dastardly bunkers that he invented a rake that purposely left deep furrows to grabbed errant balls. That rake has since been abolished with the knowledge that even with smooth surfaces, the bunkers at Oakmont are difficult enough.

One of the most unusual things about this championship golf course is that the Pennsylvania Turnpike cuts through the middle of it. But that has not hampered the reputation of Oakmont as a tournament site. Six U.S. Opens have been held there, and all have been dramatic. The memorable ones include Tommy Armour's playoff victory in 1927, Ben Hogan's win in 1953, Jack Nicklaus's defeat of Arnold Palmer in a playoff in 1962 and, of course, Johnny Miller's brilliant final-round 63 in 1973. That still stands as the course record at Oakmont, and many observers have called it the best round of golf ever played.

Miller's round came on a day when the infamous Oakmont greens were softened up by a violent tropical storm. Those greens have gained a reputation for being among the fastest—not to mention largest—anywhere. The 1935 Open champion, Sam Parks once emphatically stated that a dime he had used to mark his ball with had slid off the green!

Oakmont is certainly a grand test of golf—and surviving it, rather than beating it, is often the rule of thumb.

Playing Oakmont's 18th hole requires accuracy to avoid myriad bunkers. Johnny Miller concluded his famous 63 here in the 1973 U.S. Open.

Oak Tree

Edmond, Oklahoma

It would be hard to find a more intimidating golf course in America than Oak Tree, the somewhat demonic Oklahoma layout. Opened in 1976, Oak Tree was the brainchild of two pros from the area, Joe Walser and Ernie Vossler. The pair was determined to build a golf course capable of hosting major championships, something they felt was lacking in the state.

Pete Dye was hired to design Oak Tree, and he crafted a twisting, demanding layout. Dye has called the course the finest he has built inland. Many might say it is his best regardless.

Oak Tree begins in dramatic fashion with a 441-yard par four that demands precision off the tee. The drive must be played to the right-hand side of the fairway to avoid a clutch of trees that protects the green. That accomplished, all that remains is a midiron shot over water and sand to a severely undulating green. Unfortunately, things don't get any easier as the course unfolds.

Along with the 1st, the next three holes are often considered the key to scoring at Oak Tree. The 2nd is a 392-yard par four with water all the way down the left side. The 3rd hole is a par five of 584 yards that cannot be reached in two, and the 4th is a hefty 200-yard par three. Navigating the ball through this quartet of holes in or close to par can mean a good score, but certainly no promises can be made on the course's behalf.

Another factor that makes Oak Tree difficult is the wind. It can blow 30 kilometers on a calm day, confusing club selection and drying out greens. In those conditions, it's unlikely the course will ever be mastered.

Despite its toughness, Oak Tree has always been popular. In fact, it has had a membership waiting list dating to before it was officially opened. The course now is owned by Landmark Land Company, which has many golf properties around the world, and the oak tree that sits near the 5th tee on this course serves as the company's corporate symbol.

Oak Tree has also been a popular tournament course, hosting many local, state, and national championships. In 1988, the PGA Championships were held here, with Larry Nelson emerging as the winner.

The 16th hole, one of many with exceptionally severe results for those who miss the green.

Pete Dye, the course's architect, has called Oak Tree his finest inland course.

The Olympic Club

San Francisco, California

One of the most common strokes of a round at the Olympic Club's Lakeside course is the wood shot. This, however, should not to be confused with shots hit with a wood, but rather shots that hit wood. For trees are the most dominating of features at Olympic. Invariably, players find themselves hitting into the trees and then, consequently, playing out of them as well.

The Olympic Club has a distinguished history that dates back more than 125 years. At that time, it was founded as a downtown athletic club. In 1924, Olympic purchased the Lakeside Country Club and added it to a stable of sporting facilities offered to members. At the time, the course was wide open, but the new owners planted a virtual forest of trees that have grown up to frame each hole distinctively.

Olympic was originally designed by Wilfrid Reid with some remodeling completed in 1954 by Robert Trent Jones. Today, it stands as one of the most demanding courses on the West Coast.

At 6,700 yards, Olympic

The driver rarely comes out of the bag at Olympic when faced with tee shots such as this.

seems short, but with narrow fairways caused by the ominous trees, only a very confident player will pull the driver out of the bag with any frequency. That sacrifice of distance in favor of accuracy means the course will play longer than indicated on the scorecard.

Olympic has a wonderful history of U.S. Opens, being one of the few West Coast courses to host more than one such event. In 1955, Ben Hogan seemed assured of victory, but a birdie on the final hole by Jack Fleck forced a playoff, which Fleck won the following day.

In 1966, Arnold Palmer charged to a score of 32 on the first nine holes of the final round. Like Hogan, he seemed assured of victory, but Billy Casper equaled the score on the back nine to come from ten strokes

Olympic's narrow fair-ways, such as the 18th, can cause a golfer to play conservatively.

back to tie Palmer. The next day, Casper defeated Palmer on the tough Olympic track.

A third Open championship was held at Olympic in 1987, and Scott Simpson emerged victorious with Tom Watson as runner-up. Those two players were the only ones in the field to break par on the course.

Once on the greens, putting is no easy task, as competitors at the 1987 U.S. Open learned. Only winner Scott Simpson and runner-up Tom Watson broke par.

Pebble Beach Golf Links

Pebble Beach, California

By today's standards, it would be hard to think of Pebble Beach Golf Links as a remote and unknown golf course. But for many years after it opened in 1919, that was the case. Now, it is arguably the most renowned golf course in the world.

Pebble Beach was designed by Jack Neville, a fine California amateur golfer with no previous architectural experience. The course was built as part of a resort complex on the Monterey Peninsula on land that was used by fishermen of

Perhaps the best-known golf hole in the world is the 18th at Pebble Beach.

fishermen of Chinese descent. When completed, it attracted well-to-do summer vacationers.

But the beauty of Pebble Beach made it impossible to keep it hidden for too long. Soon it was hosting state championships, and in 1929 it welcomed the U.S. Amateur championship, in which Bobby Jones was eliminated in the first round.

Despite its name, Pebble Beach is not a proper links course. Rather than being built on the sandy links land such as that found in Scotland, it is tucked onto cliffs towering above Carmel Bay. The 4th through the 10th holes—with the exception of the 5th—along with 17 and 18, are all situated on the craggy rocks overlooking the surf. These are some of the most scenic holes in all of golf.

Television has played a great role in the notoriety of Pebble Beach. Each year the National Pro-Am is played over its layout, attracting golf's largest television audience of the season. The tournament, which gained fame thanks to promotion by Bing Crosby, is one of the most prestigious after the four majors.

While the holes that run inland are little more than routine, some of the holes at Peb-

The 7th green is located just a few feet away from the crashing waves in Carmel Bay.

The 8th hole runs along the Carmel coast and is open to the elements.

Pebble Beach, ctd.

ble Beach are as famous as the golfers who have played them. The 17th, a 209-yard par three with a green that juts out into the ocean, is ingrained in the memory of many golf lovers. On this hole, Arnold Palmer once took a nine after misjudging the wind.

There is probably no better-known hole in golf than the 18th at Pebble Beach. It is a 548-yard par five with the water on the left and out of bounds on the right. When the wind is up, the first two shots must be aimed out over the water, demanding complete faith from the golfer.

Of all the golfers who have played Pebble Beach, Jack Nicklaus must be deemed to have had the greatest success over its 18 holes. He won the U.S. Amateur here in 1961 and took the Open championship eleven years after that. He has also taken three National Pro-Am titles there.

While primarily a public golf course, Pebble Beach and the accompanying amenities were recently purchased by a Japanese firm for the reported sum of $1 billion. While that seems like a steep price, many who have enjoyed the beauties and bounty of Pebble Beach think the new owners got a bargain.

Pebble Beach is not a true links course. As the 9th hole attests, it is built above the sandy shore on rocky cliffs.

Pebble Beach was designed by Jack Neville, a fine golfer who had no experience as a course architect.

PGA West

La Quinta, California

The Stadium Course at PGA West may be the very antithesis of Scottish courses such as St. Andrews. While the latter were generally molded and shaped by the winds of time, PGA West may be the most contrived course ever built. But that does not make it a bad course. In fact, it is just the opposite.

The Stadium Course was built in 1986 by Pete Dye—with help from his wife, Alice, and Lee Schmidt—for the PGA Tour, the PGA of America, and the Landmark Land Company. More than two million yards of earth were moved and hundreds of thousands of plants brought in. The result is almost more of a sculpture than a golf course. And sitting out in the desert, it seems like a golfing oasis.

But for players, there is very little relief during a round at this course. It is one of the most difficult lay-outs in North America.

The punishment for an errant shot is severe, and on many places on the golf course there is absolutely no room for error: Either the ball lands where it should or it is gone.

While the course plays over 7,200 yards from the championship markers, the designers were not oblivious to the fact that many players of lesser abilities would not be able to play the Stadium Course. The result is that some holes have seven or eight different tees, making yardages flexible.

Still, some of the holes at PGA West are mind-boggling. Consider the 5th hole, which has a bunker 19 feet deep. It is often difficult for the golfer to get out of this bunker, let alone the ball.

Perhaps the most famous par three in America is found at the 17th, appropriately named Alcatraz. A par three, the green on this hole is an island bounded by rocks with no bail-out area. Players either hit the green or reload. Lee Trevino knows this hole well. He made an ace here in the 1987 Skins Game to pick up a huge bonus purse.

Despite the tough playing field, an invitation for a round at the Stadium Course at PGA West is unlikely to be turned down. It's just too much of a thrill to take on a course of this stature.

The 11th hole has water on the left and deep bunkers on the right. Golfers will breathe a little easier when they finally reach the green.

The bunker down the entire left side of the 16th is one of many severe penalties at PGA West.

The 17th hole is one of the most famous par threes in America. Balls are either on the green or in the water.

Pinehurst (No. 2 Course)

Pinehurst, North Carolina

While there are many testaments to the expertise of the golf course architecture of Donald Ross, his design of Pinehurst No. 2 is generally regarded to be his zenith. It is a design that has survived the test of time and continues to be highly respected by golfers of all abilities.

Pinehurst was started just prior to the turn of the century by Boston resident James Tufts as a winter getaway. After building a course to meet the demands of the guests, Tufts hired Ross as course professional in 1900. This was the beginning of a long relationship between Ross and Pinehurst, for it was less than a year after his arrival that Ross began constructing the Pinehurst No. 2 course.

Despite changes over the years, most of the origi-

nal Ross design has been recaptured in the course that exists today. Ross, of course, continually refined Pinehurst No. 2, but the flavor of the course as it was in those early days is still quite evident.

One of the major differences of the course from Ross's time has been the growth of the spindly pine trees, which line every fairway and provide a sense of peaceful isolation on each hole. The club's early history refers to Pinehurst No. 2 as more of a parkland course, but current players would have a hard time believing that.

Pinehurst, like many Ross courses, is very natural and straight ahead. There is no trickery; instead, subtle

bunkering and small greens provide the challenge. There is a premium on accuracy with approach shots and with varying lengths; players must use almost every club in their bag and often think creatively about how to get the ball in the hole.

Donald Ross's design has remained virtually unchanged since its creation back at the turn of the century.

Pinehurst's great variety means golfers will likely use every club in their bags in an attempt to tame it.

If anything distinguishes Pinehurst No. 2, it is the par-four holes. Score well on them, and the course can be beaten. But the holes offer many challenges. The 5th, for example, is a long 438 yards offering plenty of bunkers and a well-mounded green with a narrow entrance. Any chance for a birdie requires a demanding second shot often with a long iron.

Since 1901, Pinehurst has been the site of one of America's most prestigious amateur championships, the North and South Amateur. Its champions include some of golf's most distinguished players. As well, Pinehurst is a fitting site for the World Golf Hall of Fame, which opened in 1974.

Golfers who play Pinehurst No. 2 today would have a hard time believing it was once quite open. The trees have grown to add another dimension to the layout.

Pine Valley

Clementon, New Jersey

If there is a more difficult golf course in the world than Pine Valley, most golfers would not want to know of it. The New Jersey course is perennially ranked as the best in the world, and those who have had the pleasure—if it can be called that—of playing it can easily understand why.

Pine Valley's history goes back to 1912, when wealthy hotelier George Crump decided he wanted to build a golf course. He chose an area of land that was basically a forest in a swamp surrounded by sand. Crump's dream took seven years to build, and it included the removal of some twenty thousand stumps. Unfortunately for Crump, he died with only fourteen holes completed. The remaining ones, 12 through 15, were finished after his passing.

Pine Valley has no two holes that are even remotely similar. The distinctness is one of the great attractions of the course. If there is one feature that provides a common link for the holes it is the sand. Huge expanses of sand (so large they are hardly ever raked) provide both physical and mental hazards to any player.

On the 7th hole, a 585-yard par five that has never been hit in two swings, a large area of sand begins approximately 280 yards from the

Sand is the dominant element at Pine Valley. It is so prevalent that no one bothers to rake it.

The 10th hole has tough penalties for those who fail to get it on the putting surface.

Pine Valley's 17th hole is one of the reasons the course is always ranked among the best in the world.

Pine Valley, ctd.

tee and continues for another 120 yards. Even with a precise second shot, reaching the green is no easy task. It sits surrounded by more sand, and anything less than a perfect shot will leave players reaching for their sand wedges. The hole has been aptly named Hell's Half Acre.

Pine Valley continues in this fashion throughout its eighteen holes. It never gives players the opportunity for a breather. Every par three is a hit-the-green-or-else proposition. Every short par four has incredibly tough greens that are often hard to hold. Par fives also offer no easy scores. It is not uncommon to mark one or two holes in double digits for a round.

Pine Valley's difficulty is part of its history. One club member reportedly took a score of 44 on hole. Another managed to get to six under par on the first four holes thanks to a hole-in-one and a couple of chip ins. But he was so in awe of his task he never played another hole. Consider that no one broke 70 at the course from 1922 until 1939.

Pine Valley is deservedly considered the most difficult golf course in the world. One round there is the only confirmation needed.

Holes such as the 3rd explain why no one broke 70 at the course between 1922 to 1939.

Shinnecock Hills

Southampton, New York

When it comes to golf in the United States, Shinnecock Hills is a club of many firsts. It was the first eighteen-hole course in the States, the first to be incorporated, and the first in the country with a clubhouse. Shinnecock was also one of the founding clubs of the U.S.G.A., and, reputedly, the first to have a waiting list for membership. Not surprisingly, it is also one of the best tests of golf in the U.S.

Shinnecock Hills was built in 1891 for the Vanderbilts. Willie Dunn came from Scotland for the sole purpose of creating a course on the Southampton playground of the wealthy. His construction crew consisted of 150 Indians who had never seen a golf course, but they soon fashioned a twelve-hole course largely by hand. A year later, another eight holes were added.

The second U.S.G.A. championship was held at Shinnecock in 1896, and the course was humbled by many of the players. The membership did not appreciate the low scores and they began renovations, which lasted for many years, to make the layout tougher.

In 1931, William Flynn along with Howard Toomey made some major changes to the course. The result was the reputation it enjoys today as one of the strongest in the U.S. as well as its championship status.

While not a true links, Shinnecock has the feel of a Scottish course. The ocean wind and seaside grasses add challenge to the round, and the rolling terrain is reminiscent of courses across the pond.

The great variety of holes are the strength of Shinnecock. The 17th is one of the best.

For a U.S. Open course—Shinnecock hosted the 1986 championship—it is relatively short at less than 6,700 yards. But the design has factored in the prevailing winds, which force golfers to hit long irons into par fours of less than 400 yards. As well, the constant upward and downward slopes of the fairways make precision driving necessary. Hitting an errant tee shot can often mean playing the next with a difficult stance. A wonderful use of bunkers also adds to the challenge. They have been critically placed in some tricky spots; more often than not, playing a long fairway bunker shot is required during the course of a round.

The beauty of Shinnecock lies in the fact that it has such a tremendous variety of holes. It is very easy to use every club in the bag and every trick in the book to bring in a good score. Shinnecock may be old, but it is definitely still one of America's best.

The 13th usually plays into the prevailing wind, making it a difficult hole to par.

Shinnecock was the first 18-hole golf course in the United States, dating back to the 1891.

Spyglass Hill *Pebble Beach, California*

The Monterey Peninsula is known for several excellent golf courses, and while Pebble Beach and Cypress Point draw most of the attention, many golf aficionados would rate Spyglass Hill as the toughest test in that coastal area south of San Francisco.

Designed in 1966 by Robert Trent Jones, Spyglass is located on a prime area of land for a golf course. Trent Jones must have let out a cheer when he first set eyes on this ground. The breathtaking, craggy coastline meets with forests of pine and cypress. In many places on the course, the blending of these elements makes it difficult not to be distracted by the sheer beauty of the surroundings.

It would be hard to find a weak hole on Spyglass Hill. Each of the eighteen presents great physical and mental challenges to golfers of all abilities. Right from the start the course shows its teeth. The 1st hole is 600-yard par five that requires several long shots to reach the green. The hole starts in the pines and ends up near the ocean.

After a brief respite with a 350-yard par four that demands some thinking, a delicate short hole appears. The 3rd, while only 150 yards long, is most often played directly into the wind. Its green is set back in the dunes with the ocean behind.

The first few holes continue on in this fashion; all the while, the wind creates havoc with club selection. Later, the course moves back inland, but the wind is still present, leaking in and out of trees, never allowing a true read of what it is actually doing. It is not uncommon to hit a great shot only to watch it be blown many yards off line.

The greens at Spyglass are quite large and very slippery. During one round of the National Pro-Am—a PGA Tour event that utilizes Spyglass as one of the three courses—a contestant actually putted off the 15th green and into a bordering pond.

Such is the fate of those who get aggressive at Spyglass. The best advice for playing the course is to be patient. It cannot be attacked, but instead must be caressed and cajoled into surrendering a few birdies.

Like its Monterey counterparts, Spyglass is picturesque but tough. Along with Pebble Beach and Cypress Point, it is a strong member of the great Carmel triumvirate.

The mixture of coastline and forest has created a scenic masterpiece at Spyglass.

Like many holes, the 4th on the Robert Trent Jones-designed golf course is picturesque but challenging.

On the 15th, a player in the National Pro-Am actually putted off the slick green and into the pond.

The par-three 9th hole, with Lake Manassas behind the green, is among the most scenic on the course.

Robert Trent Jones

Lake Manassas, Virginia

As an architect, Robert Trent Jones has his name on many golf courses around the world. In fact, Trent Jones has designed more than 450 courses in forty-three states and thirty-four different countries in a career that has spanned nearly seventy years. There have been seventeen U.S. Opens played on courses he has built or remodeled. But not until the Robert Trent Jones International Golf Club opened in April 1991 did his name become associated officially with a course.

And as befits an architect of his magnitude, this golf course is something special. The naturally rolling terrain by the shores of Lake Manassas presents a special atmosphere that exudes golf: The land seems to have been waiting for a golf course to appear.

Jones, who of course designed the layout, called it one of the best areas of land for a golf course he'd ever seen.

From these 1,100 acres, Jones crafted a masterpiece that rates with any of his finest works. The layout is true to Jones's architectural philosophy of every hole being a hard par and an easy bogey. And with tees that allow the course to lay anywhere from 7,240 to 5,400 yards, that adage holds true for players of every handicap. The most scenic of holes comes at the 9th, a stunning par three of 199 yards that sits beside Lake Manassas. Two holes later, another wonderful par three of 185 yards appears. On this hole, the tee shot must be played directly over a large tract of the lake.

The 16th holds true to Trent Jones's belief that every hole should be a tough par but an easy bogey.

The greens at the Robert Trent Jones club are large and contoured, and most are bordered by massive bunkers.

This course is a perfect blend of tournament course and country club. Built with the hope of holding major championships, there is ample room for spectators. Yet it is a far cry from a wide-open tournament course. Instead it has an air of privacy and seclusion.

With the name of Robert Trent Jones lent to this club, it has a lot to live up to. By all accounts, it has not let the legendary architect down.

Winged Foot *Mamaroneck, New York*

Members of the Winged Foot Golf Club have for years been faced with a dilemma that many golfers would like to have: deciding which of their two courses, the East and the West, is better.

To have one excellent course at your disposal is great, but those with playing privileges at Winged Foot are blessed with two wonderful courses.

Winged Foot took its name from the emblem of the New York Ath-

Winged Foot's bunkers are deep and often require more than one stroke to get out.

Winged Foot, ctd.

letic Club, with which it was closely attached for many years. The two courses, both designed by A.W. Tillinghast, were opened in 1923 and were quickly regarded as among the best. Just six years after opening, the West course played host to the U.S. Open, which was won by Bobby Jones for the third time. Jones defeated Al Espinosa in a 36-hole playoff by an astounding 23 shots.

In 1974, after the West course was toughened up, Hale Irwin won the U.S. Open championship with a score of seven over par. If that is not a testament to the course's toughness, nothing is.

Winged Foot West course is blessed with some of the best par-four holes in golf. The scorecard shows ten par fours with distances exceeding 400 yards, seven of which are more than 440 yards. Some of the holes are unreachable in two for the average player, and those that are with-in range will likely need a solid wood shot to get home.

The 17th hole is a wonderful example of Winged Foot's par fours. The hole bends from left to right, and at the corner are four huge bunkers. Keeping the ball away from them is a tough task. The approach into the green is likely to be played with a long iron or wood, and two more huge bunkers on either side of the putting surface are ready to grab any ball straying off line.

The bunkers throughout the course are notably deep and difficult. This is certainly one of Tillinghast's trademarks, and it is unlikely anyone getting caught in these massive bunkers will forget it. Getting out of them can take more than one swing.

Winged Foot is not only a solid members course, it has also become a great tournament test, with the likes of Jones, Irwin, Billy Casper, and Fuzzy Zoeller winning Open titles there.

Winged Foot was designed by A.W. Tillinghast in 1923. It continues to offer golfers of all abilities a wonderful challenge.

The 9th hole is a straightforward hole that must still be played well to ensure a par.

Golfers standing on the green on the 5th hole are likely to feel the ocean spray in their face.

The Teeth of the Dog course skirts the ocean, forcing players to hit over the crashing waves from time to time.

Casa de Campo
La Romana
Dominican Republic

Pete Dye designed the Casa de Campo course to take advantage of the beauty of the Dominican coast.

Many golf courses around the world have been named for some fitting aspect found on its holes or some style of design. But few courses have been more appropriately named than the Teeth of the Dog course at Casa de Campo in the Dominican Republic. Indeed, this is a golf course with some bite to it.

The course was built by Pete Dye and opened in 1971. Soon after golfers began playing it, the course became recognized as one of the best in the Caribbean. Although he was not all that well known at the time, Dye, now one of golf's top architects, received a great deal of attention for the Teeth of the Dog course. To this day, Dye still owns a cottage on the property.

When it first opened, the Casa de Campo course was known both as La Romana and as Campo de Golf Cajuiles. But both these names suggested a certain calmness. *Cajuiles* is the Spanish word for "cashew," and while that name fit because of the many cashew trees throughout the course, it really wasn't suitable. So it was renamed Teeth of the Dog, a title that befits the challenges presented to golfers.

The most beautiful stretch of golf at Casa de Campo begins at the 5th hole and carries on to the 7th. These are holes that are tucked scenically against the Caribbean, and it's unlikely anyone will get through without feeling the warm spray of salt water on their faces.

The 5th is a short par three, not much more than a six or seven iron when the wind is not blowing (which is almost never). But the green is quite small and is protected by a lone tree on the right as well as rocks and sea on the left. A par here is well earned.

The 6th is a 449-yard par four with more of the ocean along the left. The 7th is another par three but of bigger proportions. From the very back, the hole can play up to 225 yards, but for most players, the short tees only 120 yards from the middle of the green are more suitable.

More of the ocean holes come on the back nine, from 15 through to 17, while the 18th is a strong finish that actually plays over an airport runway used by small island hoppers ferrying people to the resort.

In all, the Teeth of the Dog course is a beautiful and stimulating course that can easily humble the best of golfers.

Dorado Beach

Dorado, Puerto Rico

When the topics of golf and Puerto Rico are discussed, two subjects come immediately to the forefront: Dorado Beach and Chi Chi Rodriguez. While the latter, a native of this island, is known for his golfing talents and light-hearted personality, the former has made its mark as one of the great golf courses of the Caribbean.

In actuality, there are four courses at Dorado Beach. Two are situated at the Dorado Beach Hotel, while two more are just a mile down the road at the Cerromar Beach Hotel. All four were designed by Robert Trent Jones after he was commissioned by Laurance Rockefeller, the creator of the resort.

The toughest of the four courses is the Dorado East. Construction of this eighteen was not easy task. Trent Jones moved more than a million cubic yards of earth in building this championship test, mostly to reclaim swampy lands. He also flew in Bermuda grass from the mainland United States and transplanted hundreds of coconut trees. The hard work definitely paid off, as the course now is worthy of hosting any championship.

The East course is as beautiful as it is difficult. It winds its way through lush growth, over water, and beside the ocean. A player gets a little taste of everything during a round here, and the scenery sometimes hides the fact that Dorado Beach East is quite a difficult course. One of the best holes on the course is the 13th, a double-dogleg par five of some 540 yards. Water is found on both sides of the fairway, and the aggressive player may attempt to drive over it on the tee shot in hopes of reaching the green in two. But the more conservative shooter can play a series of relatively easy shots and get home in three. Jack Nicklaus has called the 13th one of the best he's ever played.

Dorado Beach was host to the 1961 World Cup, won by Sam Snead and Jimmy Demaret. For several years, it also was site of a team competition featuring LPGA and Senior PGA players. A season-ending Senior PGA Tour event was started in 1990. That is somewhat fitting, for one of the largest houses bordering the course belongs to Rodriguez, a leading player on that Senior circuit.

A little less challenging but no less enjoyable is the West Course at Dorado Beach. Holes here run haphazardly, creating havoc with players trying to judge the winds off the Atlantic. The North and South courses at Cerromar Beach round out this Caribbean golfing mecca.

Lagunita
El Hatillo County,
Miranda State, Caracas
Venezuela

The 6th hole at Lagunita flows down toward a large, undulating green protected by three large bunkers.

While South America is perhaps not known as one of the hotbeds of the golfing world, it does have pockets of excellence scattered throughout. Certainly one of those areas is found in the southeast part of the sprawling city of Caracas. Here, the Lagunita Country Club is found and—like its host country, which is rich in oil— this course is rich in design.

Conceived in 1956 and opened in 1962, Lagunita was built as part of a residential development. But unlike many other such projects, Lagunita's fairways are not lined with houses. Care has been taken to establish the course on its own and allow it to complement the area.

From its opening days, the Dick Wilson-designed course was destined to be one of Venezuela's best. The course's yardage of just more than 6,700 yards may not seem long, but at par seventy, it's a formidable challenge. The main characteristic of the course is the large and wavy greens, which are difficult to read and equally tough to putt. Expect at least a couple of three putts during a round here.

There are five par-three holes, three of which can play over 200 yards in length. The 2nd hole, a 176-yarder, is the first of the small wonders to attack. A large green is bordered by bunkers on all sides, and while it may be easy to hold, it is wrong to feel the job has been accomplished by just landing the tee shot on the putting surface. Putts of considerable distances are a regular occurrence. The 8th and 10th, holes of 211 and 208 yards, respectively, are equally as tough.

During the hosting of the 1974 World Cup, the 12th hole proved to be the most difficult for the players. The average score on this 445-yard, dogleg-right, par-four hole was 4.76. There is an out-of-bounds area stretching the entire length of the hole and a pond that protects the front of the green. A successful tee shot must favor the left side of the fairway to have a better chance at reaching the green in regulation.

The 12th was one of many challenges tackled during the World Cup and the World Team Amateurs hosted by Lagunita.

Lagunita has hosted many national and international championships, including the aforementioned World Cup, won by South Africa, and the 1986 World Team Amateur Championships, won by Canada.

Mid Ocean

Tucker's Town, Bermuda

Bermuda may be one of the world's smallest countries, but it has a very large reputation when it comes to golf. Situated on this island of 21 square miles are nine excellent golf courses, and the best of them all is the Mid Ocean Club.

Built in 1924 by Charles Blair Macdonald and remodeled in 1953 by Robert Trent Jones, Mid Ocean actually has very little ocean in its design. The majority of the holes are inland with rolling fairways and banks of scrub and bush

Mid Ocean is the top course in Bermuda, a tiny island that has become a golfing mecca.

along each side. Accuracy is a must not only on the tee shots but also the second and third strokes as well.

The 1st hole at Mid Ocean is a memorable one. With the large, majestic clubhouse behind the tee and the sprawling fairway and ocean in front, it is easy to get seduced by the beauty. The second shot on this hole can be put into the Atlantic Ocean, making for a somewhat troublesome beginning.

However, if golfers leave Mid Ocean with one memory, it is usually of the 5th hole, a 433-yard par four with a very elevated tee. From here, the golfer looks across Mangrove Lake to the fairway. It takes great judgment to determine how much of the water to cut off, and more than one greedy player has ended up wet. But the view from the teeing area is magnificent and breathtaking. A penalty stroke seems a small price to pay for the panoramic vista.

The final hole at Mid Ocean is also one of the finest on the course. Also with an elevated tee, the hole bends around the shoreline and ends in front of the clubhouse. A series of bunkers protects the green, and it takes a sharp shot to avoid them.

The par-71 course is somewhat short at 6,547 yards, but it more than makes up for that by placing a premium on course management and accuracy. In all, it takes a well-rounded game to score well at Mid Ocean.

On a romantic island dotted with pretty pink cottages and long stretches of beach, golf is almost an addiction, and Mid Ocean would certainly be the fix for anyone afflicted.

The 5th hole at Mid Ocean, with Mangrove Lake in front, is one of the most memorable.

Tryall *Montego Bay, Jamaica*

One of the most beautiful of all the Caribbean courses, the Tryall Golf and Beach Club is nestled between the ocean and Jamaica's blue-tinged mountains just outside of Montego Bay. The course, designed by American Ralph Plummer, opened as part of an exclusive resort in 1958 and has continued to improve with age.

The scenery of Tryall is exquisite. As the holes unfold, players find everything from panoramic ocean views, such as those on the 14th and 15th holes, to an old water wheel on the 6th, still working as it did many years ago when the area was a sugar plantation.

Tryall actually offers players many different golf courses. Some holes are close to the pounding surf and will be affected by swirling winds. Others are set in the mountains and will trick players with deceptive distances.

The course is lush and natural, and exotic flowers and birds seem to be everywhere. It is hard to complete 18 holes without hearing the cry of the playful koot bird, which sounds as though it is laughing at every golfer's plight.

Tryall has a good mixture of holes requiring players to produce an equally varied selection of shots. The terrain is unexpectedly hilly, and the changing elevation adds to the difficulty of club choice. A good score undoubtedly requires complete faith in the local caddies, who seem to have as many stories as the course does palm trees.

The greens are not large, but most certainly fair. There are no hidden breaks on them; what you see is what you get. But a conservative approach is often the best way to play them.

Each year, the women of the Ladies Professional Golf Association come to Tryall for their season-opening event, the Jamaica Classic. The course has proved to be a worthy test for the world's best women players and the past-champion honor roll includes Betsy King, Jane Geddes, and Patty Sheehan.

The 14th hole is one of many with great views of the ocean.

The ocean winds can cause problems with club selection on holes such as the 4th.

Tryall's lush beauty hides its great challenge. It is a rich course on this island paradise.

Europe and the British Isles

The Old Course is tucked on a thin piece of land that, more often than not, is being whipped by the wind.

Ballybunion
County Kerry,
Republic of Ireland

In the western reaches of Ireland, on the south side of the estuary of the river Shannon, sits a gem of a golf course: Ballybunion. It has been described by golf writer Herbert Warren Wind as the finest seaside course he has played. Tom Watson echoed that statement after a round there, and many lesser-known golfers—tourists from all over the world—share the opinion.

What all of them have found is as pure a course as there is nestled into a perfect setting. Standing on the first tee, the dunes stretch on in a confused pattern, never symmetrical or flat. Along the coast, white sand and ocean surf add to the magical backdrop. This is the land that makes up Ballybunion.

There are actually two courses at Ballybunion. The Old Course dates back to 1896 and was shaped by a man named Murphy with a great deal of help from Mother Nature. Over the years it has been remodeled a number of times by the likes of James Braid and Tom Simpson. The new course was fashioned by Robert Trent Jones in 1985. It is no less spectacular than the first course and looks as though it has been there for a century.

A new clubhouse at Ballybunion, built in the 1970s, accomplished many things—not the least of which was giving the membership a suitable structure. It also forced a rerouting of holes, which added to the appeal of the Old Course. Instead of finishing with two par-five holes of little charm, the course now ends with a dramatic series of a par three, par five, and two par fours (the two fives now come as the 4th and 5th holes.)

Everywhere on Ballybunion are large sand dunes, which are menacing hazards. Bunkers are used sparingly but form a critical part of the course's defense. Coupled with the relentless wind, these add up to make Ballybunion a wonderful course to attempt to navigate.

While relatively unknown outside of Ireland for decades, Ballybunion now has become a popular stop for touring golfers. A large and enchanting hotel makes it a great retreat. The two courses of exceptional quality ensure of a pleasurable golfing vacation.

There are not a great many bunkers on the course, but those that do come in to play offer a severe penalty.

The 11th hole at the Old
Course at Ballybunion
requires a careful approach.
Danger lurks on all sides.

Ballybunion's 18th hole is a
tremendous finishing test.

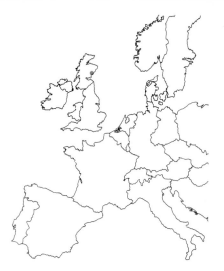

Carnoustie *Carnoustie, Scotland*

While golf has probably been played for hundreds of years on the links at Carnoustie, official records show the Carnoustie Golf Club was formed in 1839. At that time, legendary Scottish golfer Allan Robertson laid out a ten-hole course. In 1867, Old Tom Morris expanded the original design to eighteen holes, and in 1926, further changes were made under the direction of James Braid. The course had improved so dramatically that in 1931, it was awarded its first British Open championship, won by Tommy Armour.

It was following that championship that James Wright, the chairman of the Carnoustie Golf Courses Committee, headed up a group that continually made refinements to the layout. Wright's people removed bunkers, which had become outdated because of new technology, and lengthened the course to more than 7,000 yards.

In 1937, another British Open was held at Carnoustie, and it produced another memorable

The Barry Burn crosses the fairway of five holes, including three times here on the 17th.

champion: This time Henry Cotton was the victor thanks to a splendid final round of 71 shot in a torrential rain storm.

But Carnoustie's most dramatic Open came in 1953, when Ben Hogan played in his only British championship. Hogan had already won the Masters and U.S. Open that summer, but when he came to Carnoustie, he was far from the favorite because of his inexperience with British courses and the small ball then compulsory in the event. But Hogan fired rounds of 73-71-70-68 to take the title by four strokes. Gary Player conquered Carnoustie in the 1968 Open thanks in large part to a dramatic eagle at the 14th hole, and Tom Watson won in 1975.

What makes Carnoustie so tough is that each hole is so completely different from any other on the course. There are eighteen unique games for every golfer to compete against. The holes point in every direction, and the majority of them are long with or without the wind. Swirling gusts are also a factor, and determining which way they are blowing is often an impossible task. Very few golfers can say the dreaded Barry Burn, which crosses the fairway on five holes—including three times on both the 17th and 18th holes—has not had some impact on their final score.

The final holes at Carnoustie make up as fine an ending as there is in golf. The 16th, a 238-yard par three; the 17th, a 432-yard par four; and the 18th, a par four of 440 yards have decided many champions over the years. In 1931 Argentinean Jose Jurado needed to complete the last two holes in one over par to win the Open but ended up with a total of eleven. That same year, Macdonald Smith took a six on the 16th, which cost him a win.

With this history behind it, it is easy to see what makes Carnoustie such a great course.

Ben Hogan played and won his only British Open at Carnoustie.

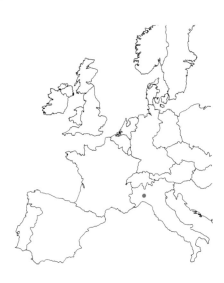

Castelconturbia
Novarra, Italy

Each year, the highlight for the growing Italian golf population comes at the Italian Open, a European PGA Tour event that brings some of the best golfers in the world to this ancient country. The chance to see players such as Nick Faldo, Ian

Woosnam, and Jose Maria Olazabal draws large crowds.

But before the tournament begins there is a healthy competition to see which course will host the event. With many excellent layouts in Italy, the bidding is tough. In 1991, the Castelconturbia was selected as the site for the tournament for the first, but likely not the last time. The response from the players and professionals was quite favorable to this graceful course.

Located near Milan, Castelconturbia is a traditional club in every sense of the word. Members here have traced the club's roots back to 1898 and are justly proud of its heritage.

Castelconturbia begins with a solid par five of 562 yards. The landing area off the tee on this dogleg right is narrowed considerably by a large bunker on the left and two trees on the right. In front of the green, three more massive bunkers appear to virtually eliminate any chance of getting home in two. This is as tough a starting hole as any player is likely to find in Europe.

The course continues in this fashion, with many holes playing tough if one gets aggressive. By playing smart rather than conservative, however, Castelconturbia can be tamed.

Three excellent finishing holes highlight this Italian course. The 16th is a good par four of some 380 yards. After a drive, most players will use an eight or nine iron to a green that is surrounded by water. At 17, a par three just shy of 200 yards, a three-iron shot to a small green is required. Getting on the green can be a tricky job, and this hole doesn't surrender too many birdies. The 18th is a 380-yard par four that most players can get close enough off the tee so they are using a nine iron or wedge for the second shot. This makes it an exciting hole, as birdies are a definite possibility.

The course record of 66 was set at Castelconturbia by Olazabal and Costantino Rocca, an Italian. Both fired the score in the fourth round of the Italian Open in 1991.

With such a magnificent course, the Italian Open will probably return to Castelconturbia. Certainly, the pros and the members wouldn't mind.

The 8th hole is better played with a conservative approach. Going aggressive is an easy way to ruin a round.

Chantilly

Chantilly, Oise, France

The town of Chantilly, 20 miles north of Paris, is best known for horse racing. But in this peaceful place, among beautiful wooded acreage, is France's best golf course, Chantilly.

The club was opened just after the turn of the century, with much of the design work being handled by Britain's Tom Simpson. Chantilly was originally composed of two courses, but during the Second World War, great damage was inflicted on the land and nine holes were abandoned. Simpson's work has undergone many changes since the end of the war, but his craftsmanship is still clearly visible today.

Chantilly is part woodland and part parkland, and it's not uncommon to see deer wandering through the course. Holes wind through the forest, much of which was planted specifically for the course, and then into the open spaces and back again. It is a splendid routing that would make an enjoyable walk even without clubs in hand.

The course opens dramatically with a long, 454-yard par four that features a large gully in front of the tee. The hole is interrupted by numerous bunkers down both sides and also around the green.

There are also strong par threes at Chantilly, with the long 14th, a 219-yard monster, being the most difficult. Bunkers surround the putting surface, and holding the green with a wood or long iron is a formidable task.

The three finishing holes at Chantilly are also quite demanding. The 16th is another long par three in excess of 200 yards. The next hole, a 425-yard par four, has more of the tremendous bunkering that is found throughout Chantilly. A series of the sandy hazards are located in the driving area on the right-hand side of the fairway and more are found at the front of the green.

The final hole is worth waiting for at Chantilly. A par five just 4 yards short of 600, the fairway rises and falls the entire distance of the hole. The green is again protected by two bunkers on each side and an accurate third shot—reaching this green in two is unlikely—is a must.

Chantilly has played host to the French Open on many occasions with such golfers as Henry Cotton, Peter Oosterhuis, and Nick Faldo emerging victorious. Like theses golfers, Chantilly is a winner.

Royal County Down
*Newcastle, County Down
Northern Ireland*

Royal County Down is one of the most memorable courses in all the United Kingdom. Set against the backdrop of the Mountains of Mourne about 50 kilometers south of Belfast, the club was formed in 1889. At that time, Old Tom Morris was contracted to lay out a course for the princely sum of four pounds. While the design has been altered over time, it is likely the members received good value for their money spent.

Royal County Down quickly earned a reputation as a strong and challenging course.

A good caddie or local knowledge is a necessity on holes such as the 9th.

Royal County Down, ctd.

In 1898, Harry Vardon defeated J.H. Taylor by 12 and 11 to win the first professional tournament played there, and both players expressed a great joy for the course. In 1908, the club was honored with the "Royal" prefix by King Edward the VII.

Royal County Down has a very strong opening hole—a 506-yard par five. This sets the tone for the remainder of the round with the golfer soon understanding the course will not lay down and be defeated. Unlike many other courses in Ireland, there are five blind tee shots to contend with and local knowledge is a definite asset. It is easy to stray into difficulty without some good advice from a caddie. But despite the unusual design, the course seems strangely proper. Once acclimatized to the flow, the golfer will find that each and every hole seems to fit like pieces to a big puzzle.

The 4th hole is one of the strongest of the first nine. A majestic par three of 217 yards, the green appears like a tiny oasis amid a desert of gorse and tangled grasses. Being short of the green can almost certainly lead to the stroke and distance penalty of a lost ball.

Royal County Down ends as it begins with a 545-yard par five. More than twenty bunkers punctuate the hole, including a grouping that appears in the middle of the fairway halfway from the green.

Many national and international tournaments have been contested over Royal County Down. The list of champions is long and impressive, but almost all would state it is the course that always ends up the winner.

The 4th hole, one of the strongest on the course, leaves little room for error.

With the Mountains of Mourne in the background, Royal County Down is one of the world's most memorable golf courses.

Royal Dornoch
Dornoch, Sutherland, Scotland

It might be easy to stand on the first tee of Royal Dornoch Golf Club and wonder if ancient gods had been the designers of this course. The sheer radiance and charm of the holes in front seem to suggest a higher being.

In truth, golf over the links of Dornoch can be traced back to 1616, and many believe it was played prior to that. But it wasn't until the late 1800s that the club was formally initiated. Shortly thereafter, Old Tom Morris was hired to lay out nine holes and a few years later, returned to add nine more.

The course has undergone some alterations over the years at the hands of John Sutherland (the club's secretary for more than fifty years), Donald Ross, and J.H. Taylor. However, with the exception of a few adjustments based more on new technology, the design has remained largely intact over the past half century, with Mother Nature shaping most of the changes.

A traditional links course in every sense of the word, Royal Dornoch is an experience to contest. Play on the course is most often dictated by the wind, and what may appear as a straightforward hole will require much contemplation. Course strategy becomes as essential a golf tool as a putter. Knowing where to hit your shot and how to hit it is usually the only combination that will lead to success.

Royal Dornoch has disappointed few and pleased many. Tom Watson once came to play a round and enjoyed it so much, he stayed for two more. American writer Herbert Warren Wind described it as having charm and character. Countless other have encountered its grace and returned to their part of the world to spread the gospel.

As with all true links courses, Royal Dornoch is constantly ravaged by the wind. The 6th and 11th holes are two where club selection varies with the breeze.

The frank beauty of the course is expressed on holes such as the 5th.

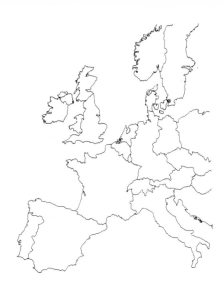

Falsterbo
Falsterbo, Fack, Sweden

Falsterbo is one of very few true links courses on mainland Europe.

Sweden is not generally thought of as country of great golf courses. In recent years, however, it has produced some excellent players, such as U.S. Women's Open champion Liselotte Neumann and top European Tour golfers Mats Lanner and Anders Forsbrand.

Just as these fine golfers were once unknown, so were Sweden's courses. Now, however, the layouts are receiving praise. Perhaps chief among the recipients of the accolades is Falsterbo, found in the Southwest corner of the country, not far from Danish capital of Copenhagen.

The first nine holes of the course were laid out for a mere $150 in 1909. In 1930, two major turning points in the club's history took place: The course was expanded to eighteen holes, and cattle and horses were banned from the area.

For the most part, Falsterbo has remained virtually intact following alterations in 1934. Natural elements have made some changes, such as on the 17th, which has been reduced to a par four because the encroaching sea swallowed the original teeing area.

Falsterbo is a true links course, one of the few on the mainland of Europe. The sea also takes over fairways on the lowlands during the winter months, which limits the club's annual Boxing Day competition to eleven holes (that has as much to do with the postgolf "glogg" party as it does with unplayable lies).

The signature of the club is an old lighthouse, which sits near the 14th green. It acts as a beacon not only for seafaring vessels, but for desperate golfers who can eas-

ily lose their way on this challenging course.

Falsterbo is full of hazards, both sand and water. There are ninety-two large bunkers waiting to grab unsuspecting golf balls, and a majority of the holes have some type of natural water menace. After negotiating through those and onto the greens, putting can be tough in the slick greens.

The final two holes at Falsterbo present a dramatic finish to any round. The tee shot at 378-yard 17th leaves from the tip of the peninsula on which the course is situated and travels down a fairway marked by two well-placed bunkers and a small pond. From there, the approach shot is to a long green, which has two more bunkers acting as sentries for incoming balls.

The 18th is a good par five measuring close to 500 yards. The tee shot must be kept left, and the sweeping wind will aid in this task almost to a detriment. Reaching the green in two is possible but difficult. A birdie here is well earned.

In 1930, Falsterbo expanded to eighteen holes and banned cattle and horses from the property.

Muirfield:
The Honourable Company of Edinburgh Golfers
Muirfield, Lothian Scotland

The records of the Honourable Company of Edinburgh Golfers can be traced back continuously to 1744. This makes it the oldest golf club in existence, although there are some who still dispute this claim. But it is safe to say it was in operation a full ten years before the Royal And Ancient. In fact, when St. Andrews drew up its rules, it actually adopted verbatim the Honourable Company's famous "13 Articles," a code established for playing golf.

The club's first playing ground consisted of five holes on the links at Leith. When that land became crowded, it moved to Musselburgh. Finally, in 1891, the Company relocated down the Firth of Forth at Muirfield. The rest, as they say, is history, for many great moments have occurred over the Muirfield course.

The 1892 British Open played there was the first to be contested over seventy-two holes, doubling from the previous thirty-six. This also makes Muirfield the oldest

Open championship course still being used today. Harry Vardon won the Open title at Muirfield in 1896 by defeating J.H Taylor in a playoff. The list of other Open champions at Muirfield reads like a Who's Who of golf: Hagen, Cotton, Player, Nicklaus, Trevino, Watson, and Faldo. All great players who were able to conquer the magnificent course.

Muirfield does not resemble many other Scottish links courses, partly because it does not get as close to the sea. It is much flatter a course and is laid out in two loops. The first nine holes move clockwise on the outside edge of the land, while the second nine follow a counter-clockwise direction on the inside. This makes the course wonderful

Muirfield, as shown here on the 2nd hole, is a much flatter course than ts Scottish counterparts.

95

Muirfield, ctd.

for spectators, who can get to almost any hole on the course in a matter of a few minutes.

What also sets Muirfield apart from its Scottish counterparts is the lack of hidden hazards. There are no bunkers lurking to grab errant shots and no sudden changes in direction that may mislead. From the clubhouse, the entire course can be seen, open and spacious, yet still quite private.

This is not to suggest that Muirfield is an easy course—far from it. There is plenty of trouble waiting for the golfer who strays from the fairway in the form of long, matted grass, which often prevents a player from doing anything more than just pitching back to the fairway.

The bunkers that protect the greens—as well as numerous others that seem to be devilishly placed some 50 yards from the putting surfaces on most holes—are marvelously strategic.

The course is as fair as championship golf gets. And with its impressive list of tournaments and tournament winners, it would be safe to place it among the best in that category.

Although it moved several times in its early days, Muirfield was in operation a full ten years before St. Andrews. The present clubhouse is a worthy home of golf's oldest club.

The bunkers, such as these on the 13th, are cruel but usually not hidden from view.

Portmarnock

Portmarnock, County Down Republic of Ireland

On a small peninsula of land that juts into the Irish Sea can be found one of golf's most naturally glorious courses, Portmarnock. Here is a course that has received accolades from some of the world's finest golfers. Any who came with doubts left in awe of one of Ireland's best tests of golf.

Portmarnock was started by a Scotsman living in Dublin, W.C. Pickeman, who teamed up with George Ross, a scratch player, in hopes of starting a golf club. The two traveled by boat to the spit of land and leased some fields, upon which they laid out nine holes. A shack rented from a Maggie Leonard served as the initial clubhouse and, with the only potential problem being Leonard's cow (which developed a voracious appetite for golf balls), the club was established.

Over the years, many different architects have had a hand in designing holes at Portmarnock, but with the natural elements affecting the course daily, it might be more appropriate to say the course evolved.

These same elements are what determines how a round is played at this fine Irish links. Surrounded by water on three sides, the course is almost always affected by wind. Sometimes it is a gentle breeze, while other times it is a full-force gale. When the wind howls, three strong shots can still leave a player short on par fives, such as the 550-yard 6th. When hitting with the wind, distance is rarely a problem.

The par-three holes at Portmarnock are all devilishly delightful. The 15th, a 191-yard gem, is situated close to the sea. A blowing wind forces players to aim out into the water and hope the ball will be brought back to the green. Nerves of steel are a definite prerequisite.

Portmarnock has been a popular championship tournament site. In August 1927, the course hosted the first Irish Open with the prize money of 100 pounds donated by the members. George Duncan claimed the title after firing a 72 in the last round during a gale that blew away all the tents.

In 1960, Arnold Palmer and Sam Snead teamed up to capture the World Cup (then Canada Cup) title at Portmarnock by a healthy eight shots.

The 12th green at Portmarnock necessitates a well-placed approach shot. The bunkers that flank the putting surface spell certain bogey.

Quinta da Marinha

Cascais, Portugal

One of the most picturesque resorts in Europe is the Quinta da Marinha, overlooking the Atlantic Ocean on the Estoril Coast. Tucked into a pine forest on a vast private estate, the unspoiled surroundings bring true meaning to serenity.

The course was designed by Robert Trent Jones in 1985 and has an exciting make up of six par threes, six par fours, and six par fives. This makes for a challenging round and presents an opportunity to attack the course.

At 6,600 yards, Marinha is not exceptionally long, but the par-seventy-one course has a great deal of trouble that must be avoided if a good score is to be recorded. Holes such as the par-three fifth are a good example. At 185 yards, the tee shot must carry a pond that covers almost all the area between the tee and green. Just in front of the putting surface is a collection of five bunkers that grab more than their fair share of balls. Once on the green, the job is far from over as swales and breaks are everywhere.

The 10th hole is another exhilarating one. A par five of 520 yards, it has a fairway that is bordered by water on both sides. The daring players may attempt to hit the green in two, but any shot even the slightest bit short will find the water. It is a wonderful example of a risk-reward shot.

Most of the holes on the course are open enough that the driver can come out of the bag. But the smart player may choose to lay up in favor of accuracy as positioning off the tee is a key to a good score.

With the course built onto cliffs overlooking the Atlantic, Marinha has some exceptionally pretty panoramas. It is easy to forget a high score when viewing the scenery offered during a round. Perhaps this is why this Portuguese course remains one of the most popular for vacationers from all over the world.

Marinha's greens have never been called unfair. They are large enough to be receptive to incoming shots, but with numerous swales and undulations, tricky enough to require special attention when lining up putts.

A number of holes on the Estoril coast overlook the Atlantic. Even with a poor score, the scenery is enough to make a round worthwhile

Royal and Ancient
Golf Club of St. Andrews (The Old Course)

St. Andrews, Fife, Scotland

Since the earliest days of the game, golfers the world over have looked to St. Andrews as their holiest shrine. It has become their Mecca, the castle of the kingdom, the home of golf.

The distinguished reputation of St. Andrews is almost a curious one to those who have played the course. There is nothing fancy about the Old Course. It has no tricks, no gimmicks, no railway ties or fountains. The attraction is the uncorrupted purity. More than anywhere else in the world, this is golf. It is natural and awe inspiring, as it should be.

The earliest records indicate golf has been played at St. Andrews for more than four centuries. In its infancy, golfers played eleven holes out and the same eleven back again, for a round of twenty-two holes. In the mid-1700s, however, the first four holes were combined into two and a round consisted of eighteen

One of the most famous finishes in golf: the 18th at St. Andrews with the Swilcan bridge.

The 1st hole and 2nd tee of St. Andrews at sunrise.

St. Andrews, ctd.

holes. It is this format that caused eighteen to become the standard for golf courses around the world.

St. Andrews is located on a thin strip of land that at times hardly seems wide enough to hold a championship golf course. On fourteen of the holes there are large double greens. An interesting note is that the sum of any two holes sharing a green totals eighteen. The greens, which sit up above the fairways, are usually hard from the constant breezes off the shore, making it difficult to land and stay with lofted approach shots. The pitch and run is often the only solution. The fairways are now the beneficiaries of an automatic watering system, but in days gone by, tee shots would seemingly roll forever on the firm ground.

The 14th hole exudes the natural and raw feeling of the Old Course.

The two major problems with any round at St. Andrews are the wind and the bunkers. The wind can swirl and gust at such tempos as to never give players an advantageous hole. The bunkers, which are distinguished with names such as Hell's Bunker and the Beardies, are a little more predictable, but not any more beneficial to a scorecard.

St. Andrews is also the home of the Royal and Ancient, the governing body to the game in most parts of the world. Here, rules are determined and policies set. The organization has served as golf's guiding hand.

The course's tournament history is too long to discuss in detail, but most of the great champions have had their day here. Many a memorable moment has taken place over the links of St. Andrews. Rest assured many more will occur on this hallowed garden of golf.

There are no gimmicks or tricks on the Old Course. The simplicity is its attraction.

Sotogrande *Sotogrande, Cadiz, Spain*

In North America, the phenomenon of golf courses being built in conjunction with real estate developments is old hat, an accepted fact. A house on a golf course is one of the most desirable homes. But in Europe, the first such course did not appear until the mid-1960s. It was Sotogrande, on Spain's Costa del Sol—and with the growing reputation of the golf course, it would be fair to say the home owners made a good buy.

Sotogrande was also the first venture in Europe for legendary architect Robert Trent Jones. His influence is clearly seen at this Spanish layout. Built from an area of sandy fields and cork trees in 1964, the course has many panoramic views of Gibraltar, just 20 miles to the north.

Sotogrande begins calmly, much like the surrounding land. A straight-away par four of just less than 400 yards is a good begin-ning to the following challenges. The most dramatic hole comes at the 7th, where the tee shot must be played into a valley. On the second shot, golfers must navigate the woods to the left and water on the right in hopes of landing on the green.

The 14th hole is another great challenge. A par-five, dogleg left of some 500 yards, the tee shot is played over one of several artificial lakes on the course to a relatively narrow but ever-widening fairway. The green is guarded with trees on the left of the green and several bunkers on both sides of the putting surface.

At the finish is another wonderful golf hole, a strong finale to a round at Sotogrande. The 18th is 440 yards of gently rising fairway and again, the green is fronted by a series of bunkers. An accurate second shot, generally with a long iron, is needed to have any chance of a birdie.

A little more than ten years after the original course was built, Trent Jones returned to Sotogrande to add another eighteen. It has many similarities to the Old Course but may lack a little of the character. Time, however, may cure that.

Many real estate courses may have a somewhat tainted reputation, being built more as a sales tool than anything else, but Sotogrande is not among them. It can stand proudly on its own.

The 15th hole at Sotogrande's Old Course is guarded by four bunkers. The shot to the green must be exact to avoid them.

Sunningdale

Ascot, Berkshire England

At the start of this century there existed a strip of wasteland outside of London that most people believed to be quite useless. It was barren and rough with the exception of some shrubs of little consequence. But it soon became apparent that the land would be wonderful for golf courses. Today, some of England's finest layouts exist in this heathland. The best of all of these courses is undoubtedly Sunningdale.

The Old Course at Sunningdale got its start shortly after the turn of the century. The land upon which it is today situated was owned by St. John's College, Cam-

Prior to the Second World War, Sunningdale played host to royalty and was regularly visited by British socialites. Today, its clubhouse and course are still quite regal.

Sunningdale, ctd.

bridge, which granted a lease for development of the course to two brothers, George and T.A. Roberts. They quickly hired Willie Park Jr., the 1887 and 1889 British Open winner who went on to become one of the greats of golf architecture. At the time, however, he was still making a name for himself in the design business. At Sunningdale, he built the foundation to a great golf course that was fine-tuned by Harry Colt in 1922.

Prior to the outbreak of the Second World War, Sunningdale was a very fashionable place to be. Members of the royal family often played there, and tournaments were integrated as part of the social scene of the day.

While the club obviously suffered during the war years, the craters caused by German bombs were later filled with sand and used as bunkers. While they would never know it, the Luftwaffe is another of the great architects who has touched up Sunningdale over the years. Today, Sunningdale is a course full of charm and elegance. It is never brash, but rather quietly deceiving. Golfers soon realize, however, that despite is straightforward appearance, it does have some bite. Many greens are raised and well protected. This usually means the short irons must be extremely accurate. An errant pitch can quickly run off the green and into a bunker. Putting can also be tricky, with breaks that don't seem to be there suddenly appearing.

Some impressive rounds have been played at Sunningdale. Australian Norman Von Nida shot a final-round 63 to win the Dunlop Masters just after the war, and in 1956, Gary Player took the same tournament after shooting a 64.

The European Open has been held regularly at Sunningdale, being played there seven times in a nine-year period beginning in 1982. The winners have included such players as Ian Woosnam, Bernhard Langer, Greg Norman, and Isao Aoki.

The 10th hole offers a simple but challenging start to the back nine.

Royal Troon

Troon, Strathclyde

Scotland

The 11th hole at Troon presents an open but wind-swept challenge.

The Royal Troon Golf Club began as a five-hole course on land leased from the sixth Duke of Portland back in 1878. The small but avid group of golfers who inaugurated the course could have no idea at the time that it would become one of the best tests of the game in all of Scotland. Today, Royal Troon is among the most demanding of courses for the high handicapper and for the world's best, who attempt to tackle it during British Open championships.

Because of the popularity of the Troon course, the original five holes grew to six, then twelve and finally, in 1888, there were eighteen holes designed by Willie Fernie, the long-time pro greenskeeper of the club. And since 1904, when it hosted the British Ladies' Amateur Championship, it has been a favorite site for championships.

Royal Troon has one of the longest and one of the shortest holes in British championship golf. The 6th, a 577-yard par five, is usually played into the prevailing wind. The hole is virtually unreachable in two for the average player and only a conservative approach will yield a par.

On the scorecard, the 8th, a 125-yard par three, doesn't seem intimidating. But when it is viewed from the tee, hearts usually skip a beat. Known as the Postage Stamp (although the hole's real name is Ailsa), the 8th at Royal Troon was built in 1910, replacing the original hole, a 292-yarder that featured a blind shot to a green. After being unveiled to the membership, there was much consternation, as it was thought to be too difficult. Some players went as far as to call it the worst golf hole ever seen. But the hole was praised by a group of distinguished pros, including Harry Vardon and J.H. Taylor, following an exhibition match. It has gone on to become one of the best-known holes in the world.

In the 1950 British Open, a German amateur, Hermann Tissies, hit his shot in the bunker on the left and finally extracted it after five swipes. But his ball ended up in a bunker on the other side of the green, which required another five strokes before he sent the ball back to the original bunker. He ended up with a fifteen on his card. A little more successful was Gene Sarazen, who at age seventy-three, made an ace at the Postage Stamp.

Troon has hosted the British Open on six occasions, the most recent coming in 1989, when a new, three-hole playoff format saw Mark Calcavecchia steal the title away from Greg Norman and Wayne Grady.

The Postage Stamp is among golf's most famous— and difficult—par threes.

Turnberry

Turnberry,

Strathclyde

Scotland

Although it hardly seems possible now, during the Second World War, the course was transformed into an air base with several runways.

The story of the famous Turnberry (Ailsa) course is as much a story of survival as anything else. For it was not that long ago that many people felt golf would never be played a Turnberry again. But today, the championship course at the great hotel is one of the most revered in all of golf.

As golf courses in Scotland go, Turnberry is relatively young, having been built by Willie Fernie, the professional at Troon for many years, in 1909. Two courses were constructed, the Ailsa, regarded as the better of the pair, and Arran. Soon after their completion, golfers were flocking to play them and stay at the luxurious hotel.

When war broke out in 1914, the air force took over the course and used it as a training ground for Commonwealth fliers. A memorial to the dead pilots can be seen by the 12th green of the Ailsa course.

Following the war, the courses were repaired and flourished for a number of years, but with the outbreak of the Second World War, the pilots again took over. An entire air base was constructed on the course with runways 18 inches thick with cement. It was at this point that many felt the site would never again return to the golfing mecca it once was.

However, after some strong negotiating by the hotel manage-

Turnberry's signatures are the lighthouse and the view of Ailsa Craig.

Turnberry, ctd.

ment, the government was obliged to put up funds to rebuild the courses to an even more magnificent stature than before the war. By 1951, Turnberry was once again a popular golfing destination, thanks largely to the great work of Mackenzie Ross, who shaped new holes with tribute to the old ones. It became host to many tournaments, such as the Walker Cup and the British Amateur, but it was in 1977 that the Ailsa course received its crowning glory as site of the 106th British Open Championship.

That event was one of golf's greatest tournaments, with Tom Watson and Jack Nicklaus scoring identical rounds of 68, 70, and 66, before teeing off together in the final round. That day, Watson outdueled Nicklaus 65 to 66 in a memorable finale.

In 1986, Greg Norman mastered the Turnberry course—including the difficulty presented by the elements—from start to finish to capture the British Open.

Whether a golfer is contesting an Open championship or a $2 nassau, Turnberry is a sight to behold. The great granite of Ailsa Craig sits in the waters while Arran's mountains rise up behind. The panoramic views are only hindered by the heavy weather, which can come and go quite unpredictably.

If for no other reason than perseverance, Turnberry should be on every Scottish visitor's itinerary. Its long battle to survive has been rewarded with its place among golf's great courses.

The 16th hole and its dramatic green are part of the great traditions at Turnberry.

The 14th hole and the rest of Turnberry have challenged high handicappers and British Open champions, including Tom Watson and Greg Norman.

Vilamoura

Algarve, Portugal

The umbrella pines on the 9th act as a narrow border on all shots.

Although it only opened in the late 1960s, Vilamoura has the look of a very mature course.

For many years, vacationers have been coming to the Algarve to soak up the sun and enjoy the good life. But until the late 1960s, these travelers could not enjoy any golf of which to speak. That all changed in 1969, when the Vilamoura Golf Club opened for play. Excellent golf was soon on the itinerary of the many visitors who came to this part of Portugal.

The Vilamoura development was started by Artur Cupertino de Miranda, who in 1964, acquired a large estate. He then founded Lusotur, a company whose sole intention was to make this land into a resort second to none.

Actually the third of the Algarve courses to open, Vilamoura's first golf course, (there are three 18s here) was built by British architect Frank Pennick, who was given a choice of three sites in the large expanse of some 4,000 acres. The land was light and sandy, making it ideal for course construction, and Pennick made good use of the property in his work.

Vilamoura has a distinctly British feel, as holes sweep down and away from the start. Some holes are on steep grades, while others are more level but always gently undulating. Umbrella pines and cork trees line much of the layout, significantly narrowing many fairways but not totally obscuring the beautiful ocean views. Overall, there is great variety to the eighteen holes at Vilamoura. It makes for an interesting round that calls for every shot in the bag.

The course plays a little more than 6,500 yards with a par of 73. Perhaps the most challenging of holes at Vilamoura are the par threes. The first of these shorter holes comes at the 4th, a 168-yarder over a lake. The water, which rests halfway between the green and tee, shouldn't really come into play, but a large tree at the right side of the hole does. Depending on the pin placement, it protects a portion of the green, as do bunkers at the front and sides of the hole. While extremely pretty, the 4th is deceivingly tough and requires an accurate touch for any chance at a par.

The other par-three holes are equally challenging and demand precision from the tee.

As a resort course, Vilamoura hasn't had too many tournaments on its layout, but the Algarve and Portuguese Opens as well as the World Ladies Amateur Championships have all been played here at one time or another.

While the original course still provides the best test of golf at Vilamoura, a second eighteen, also designed by Pennick, was added in 1976. Robert Trent Jones made renovations at both courses in 1985. In 1990, a third layout was added, this time crafted by American architect Joe Lee.

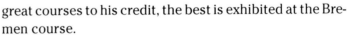

Club Zur Vahr
Bremen, Germany

The city of Bremen in northern Germany is situated on the banks of the Weser River, 40 miles from the North Sea. As the second-largest port city in Germany, it is also the commercial center for the northern part of this country. But for golfers, Bremen is home to one of Germany's best golf courses, the Club Zur Vahr.

Although golf in Bremen dates back to the turn of the century, the present course was built in 1966 by Bernhard von Limburger, the most prolific of German architects. Limburger was a strong proponent of strategic designs and disliked water hazards and excessive bunkering. From this came a distinctive style, which is seen at many German courses. The best testament to his work is that every German Open after the Second World War until 1978 was played on a Limburger course. While he has many great courses to his credit, the best is exhibited at the Bremen course.

The Club Zur Vahr is a multisports facility, and it was the decision of the membership to build a course worthy of championship play. A spot in the Garlstedter Heath was chosen and seemed perfect for the members' needs. It was 220 acres of densely forested land that rises and falls throughout. So thick were the trees that the original design had only twenty-four bunkers on it. Any more would not be necessary.

The course has not changed since its opening, except that the trees are, of course, much taller and thicker. This presents a testy situation for most players, as not only is Club Zur Vahr narrow but also quite long. From the back tees, it stretches to more than 7,200 yards. There are six par-five holes on the par-seventy-four course, all of them over 500 yards. So not only must golfers be accurate, but also long.

First and foremost, Zur Vahr is a driving course. Every tee shot must be played with great care. Because of the many doglegs, ending up on the wrong side of the fairway means a hook or a cut is almost always required. But a player who gets off the tee well can expect to have a good chance at a low score.

Club Zur Vahr is a natural and scenic course. As a tournament site, it has been the host to the German Open. With time, it will continue to improve in both beauty and challenge.

The trees and doglegs mean position off the tee is of the utmost importance at Club Zur Vahr.

Zur Vahr was cut out of dense forests that provide so much protection, only twenty-four bunkers were included in the original design.

115

Asia, Australasia, and South Africa

The rolling fairway on the 18th hole at New South Wales in Australia provides a wonderful finishing test.

Bali Handara Kosaido

Pancasari, Bali, Indonesia

Bali lies at the eastern end of the Indonesian archipelago, about as far from the roots of golf as one can go. But hidden in a valley a couple of hours from the city of Denpasar is the unlikely golf jewel known as Bali Handara.

Designed by Australian great Peter Thomson, the course is surrounded by lush rain forest. Tropical flowers produce an incredible range of pigments on every hole, and the smell of the flora fills the air. There is so much beauty at Bali Handara, it is often easy to forget one is on a golf course and not in a rich garden.

Because of an almost complete lack of machinery and some extremely wet periods during the year (more than an inch of rain per day is not unusual), constructing Bali Handara was a demanding task. Not only did rain hamper work conditions, but building a course that could handle it in such proportions was no easy job. Fortunately, the use of specially selected grasses and natural drainage patterns have kept Bali Handara in consistently good condition, despite facing some terrible weather.

The course is as enjoyable to play as it is to behold. Bali Handara plays somewhat shorter than the 7,000 yards listed on the scorecard because of its location 4,000 feet above sea level. However, it is still beneficial to be long off the tee. The 18th hole, at 560 yards, is the longest on the course and a strong finishing test. All four par threes measure 180 yards, although each is unique in appearance. It is rare to use the same club on even two of them.

Bali Handara's bag tags describe the course as "one of the world's great courses." With the surrounding beauty and exceptional golf course, it is an accurate claim.

Bali Handara utilized special grasses and natural drainage to contend with the heavy rainfalls it receives. The course is easily able to handle the wet weather.

Designed by Peter Thomson, the great Australian professional, Bali Handara is surrounded by lush rain forest.

Durban

Durban, Natal, South Africa

The Durban Country Club was built in 1923 by Laurie Waters, known as the father of South African Golf. Waters emigrated to South Africa from his native St. Andrews, where he apprenticed under Old Tom Morris. He went on to win the first South African Open, introduced grass greens to the country, and laid out several golf courses. By many accounts, Durban Country Club is his finest effort.

The course was constructed into the sandhills that are found near the seashore south of the Umgeni River. It has changed little since its early days and now is regarded as one of the best tournament courses in South Africa. It has been host to almost every national championship and can claim such winners as Bobby Locke, Bobby Cole, and Gary Player.

The professional course record is held by Cole, who scored a wonderful 63 during the 1980 South African Open. He went on to win the

The 2nd hole forms part of the "Famous Five," the first five holes at Durban, which have been the downfall of many.

Built in 1923, the Durban Country Club has seen the surrounding area grow over the years. Large trees still provide a secluded atmosphere for golfers.

tournament with a four-round total of 279, one of very few times players have broken 280 in competition.

Durban Country Club is not long, playing only a little more than 6,600 yards. But the wind combined with narrow fairways makes the course a difficult test for even the best of golfers. The 1st hole is an excellent example of the challenges Durban presents. From an elevated tee, players must drive between dense brush on the left side and a bunker and out of bounds on the right. When the hole plays into the wind, a tee shot that finds the fairway will likely rest on a downhill slope, making the approach that much more difficult. With the wind, it can be as little as a nine iron to the green.

At the other end of the round, the 18th hole may be among the shortest of any championships golf course. But that doesn't mean it is easy to score on it. The hole is 273 yards in length and features the picturesque, gabled clubhouse in the distance. Most players will attempt to drive the green but usually end up in trouble. The fairway is tight with many undulations, and a wayward drive can end up in a thick patch of scrub on the left or down a steep hill to the practice area on the right. It makes for an interesting finish to a round at a lovely golf course.

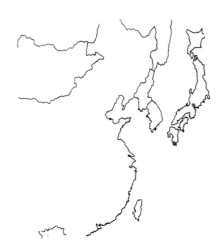

Fujioka *Nagoya, Japan*

Perhaps the most unusual thing about the beautiful Fujioka Country Club is that unlike most other Japanese courses, it is usually not very busy. That is not so much because no one wants to play it, but rather that the membership is strictly limited. Only 520 members are allowed, and judging by the course, they are very lucky indeed.

Fujioka Country Club opened for play in 1971 after being designed by Peter Thomson and Michael Wolveridge. The two architects had a marvelous piece of land with which to work: 180 acres of what was a tea plantation accented by a large lake.

The result has been a distinctive course with many features not usually found in Japanese layouts.

The most distinguishing trait is the use of water, which is traditionally employed more for beauty than hazards in Japan. But at Fujioka, greens are buttressed by ponds and being off slightly in direction can mean getting wet.

The most unusual hole at Fujioka is surely the 12th, a good example of the liquid hazard. The hole is actually two holes with two separate greens. One hole is played as a dogleg left with a green protected by water, while the other is more traditional, being straight ahead with a couple of bunkers serving as the only hazard. The finishing holes at Fujioka are dramatic and diffi-

Fujioka, unlike many other Japanese courses, has a strictly limited membership of 520. This makes it one of the least crowded clubs in that country.

cult. A championship would certainly have a fitting finale on this trio.

The 16th is a monster, 605-yard par five that rises continually up until the green, which is guarded by water on one side and sand on the other. On 17, the tee shot must carry 195 yards over the largest lake on the golf course property to a landing area with two distinct halves. A lone tree divides the fairway, which has split levels on either side, one higher than the other. The 18th is a par four of 430 yards. The tee shot is to a wide fairway, but the approach shot must carry a creek and avoid the lake banking the left side of the fairway.

While Fujioka is not a typical Japanese golf course, it is not to be discounted. It is one of that Asian country's best.

Cherry blossoms grace the 2nd hole at Fujioka.

Fujioka, ctd.

Tee shots on the 18th must be kept right to avoid the water on the left side.

Royal Hong Kong

Fanling, Hong Kong

With the mountains of China rising up in the distance, the three courses of the Royal Hong Kong Golf Club are set in one of the most stunning locations for any golf course. The beauty of the surrounding area

Royal Hong Kong has survived many turbulent years to become one of the most respected courses in Asia.

is second to none and almost makes one forget about the game at hand.

The history of the Royal Hong Kong Golf Club is a testament to survival. After an unimpressive beginning back in 1889, when thirteen people answered a local newspaper advertisement about starting a golf club, Royal Hong Kong has moved several times and had to deal with flooding of the course, turf damage thanks to sharing premises with polo ponies, and the occupation of the Japanese army during the Second World War. The Japanese troops devastated the course and went so far as to use the greens as vegetable gardens. Only a strong will and determination to play golf by the members has kept the club going.

With a large membership, Royal Hong Kong makes great use of its three courses. The Old, as its name suggests, was the first to be built, opening for play in 1911. This layout has a distinctly British feel, with driving and a strong short game being almost a necessity. A wonderful stretch of holes, known as the Loop, comes between the 10th and 13th, and a match can be and certainly has

been decided here.

The New course began play in 1931 and was redesigned in 1968 by Michael Wolveridge. These holes are more like those found in the United States with wide-open fairways, especially on the second nine.

In 1970, with membership still strong, a third eighteen was built on land obtained from the Royal Hong Kong Jockey Club. During construction, many old Chinese graves were found, which created great difficulties for the club. Fortunately, matters were ironed out and another fine track was added, albeit into somewhat cramped quarters. Named Eden, after the third course at St. Andrews, this layout has some short holes as demanded by the small acreage upon which it is built. But what it lacks in yardage, it makes up for in character. The 18th, a 409-yard par four surrounded on all sides by out of bounds, is the best hole on the course and could be the toughest finishing hole in Asia.

Royal Hong Kong has hosted many championship tournaments and when these occur, a composite of the New and Eden courses is used. The combination of the two 18s is superb, as many fine professionals and amateurs will no doubt attest.

Construction of the Eden course was hampered when builders found a number of ancient Chinese graves. As the 17th hole shows, however, the problems were solved and the layout completed.

Royal Melbourne
*Black Rock, Melbourne,
Victoria, Australia*

While the Royal Melbourne Golf Club can trace its roots back to 1891, when it began play near Caulfield Station, the present site of the course—regarded by many as one of the best in the world—was not opened until 1901. At that time, the Lieutenant-Governor, Sir John Madden, christened the new course by whiffing the first shot.

That course was altered into the immaculate and incomparable design that exists today by Alister Mackenzie, the architect behind Augusta National and Cypress Point, back in 1926. The club paid Mackenzie 1,000 guineas to suggest changes, and his advice was well taken.

Royal Melbourne is regarded as one of the best courses in the world. Its classic design—virtually unchanged since 1926—has withstood the test of time.

He eventually created the masterpiece now known as the West Course, while Alex Russell, a former Australian Open winner who assisted Mackenzie with that job, went on to design the East Course.

The Royal Melbourne that is used for international tournament play is actually a composite of the two courses.

This routing was initially used in the 1959 World (then Canada) Cup to avoid several busy roads on the property.

The two designers were assisted by course superintendent Claude Crockford, who made the greens his personal testament to this golfing shrine. According to those who have played the course, they are as true and

127

This aerial view of Royal Melbourn shows its proximity to the ocean.

Rotal Melbourne, ctd.

quick as any in the world. In 1974, Lee Trevino, obviously frustrated by the lightning-quick pace on the putting surfaces, stormed off the course and vowed never to return. He was not the first or last to make that promise after a devastating round.

Royal Melbourne has many signature holes, but perhaps the par threes are among the most memorable. The 5th, for example, a 176-yard marvel, plays across a valley of heather and scrub to a heavily bunkered green. At the front of the green is a steep slope back into the valley that will catch any ball minutely short of the putting surface. And with the slope of the green going from front to back, long shots tend to run to the far side of the green.

Another wonderful par three is found at the 210-yard 16th. It requires a long iron or wood to an elevated green that is protected on the left by a sand trap.

Trevino aside, first-time players at Royal Melbourne are usually humbled. But they can quickly understand why this course is regarded as one of the world's best.

Royal Melbourne's natural beauty can sometimes lull golfers' thoughts away from the task at hand.

The 5th hole at Royal Melbourne, a 176-yard par three, plays across a valley of scrub and brush to a well-bunkered green.

New South Wales
La Perouse, New South Wales, Australia

It might be proper to call the New South Wales Golf Club the most Australian of all courses Down Under. After all, it is located only a few hundred yards away from the spot where Captain Cook landed in the *Endeavour* in 1770 and "discovered" this country.

Adventurers who travel to this part of the continent now will discover a fine golf course with a definite links feel. The New South Wales Golf Club may not be the most difficult of Australian golf courses, but it certainly among the most picturesque. The Pacific Ocean laps at its doorstep, and gently rolling hills spread out in all directions. It is a visual treat whether one is playing the course or not.

The club was designed by Alister Mackenzie, who took some acres of thick scrubland leased from the Australian Army and transformed it into a delightful course that has remained true to the original layout. It was opened in 1928 by the Australian Governor General of the day, the Right Honorable Baron Stonhaven.

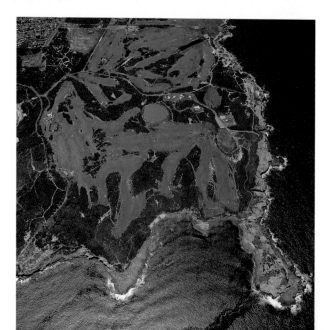

*New South Wales Golf Club is located a few hundred yards from the spot where Captain Cook landed in the **Endeavour.***

From any view, the New South Wales Golf Club is spectacular.

Unfortunately, fourteen years after this impressive opening, the army reclaimed the land and clubhouse for war preparation. As might be expected, when it was returned to the members, it bore little resemblance to the exquisite golf course of earlier times. But with a strong effort on the part of the membership it soon returned to its original state. Not long after, the Australian Amateur Championship was held at New South Wales, signaling its official rebirth among the country's great courses.

The signature hole at New South Wales is undoubtedly the 6th. Unlike many courses that now feature an island green, this hole has an island tee, which is set back on the craggy rocks of the ocean. At 196 yards, it is a good test in addition to being a scenic delight.

On almost every hole, the wind acts as an invisible hazard, playing havoc with club selection and shot direction. The difficult greens also add to the improbability a low score. New South Wales is richly beautiful and a treat to play.

The 6th hole is the course's signature, with the championship tee set back on the craggy rock peninsula.

Paraparaumu
Beach *Wellington*
New Zealand

About 45 kilometers north
of the New Zealand capital
of Wellington lies a seaside
course that truly is at one with its surroundings. The sea air, with its
salty aroma, is a constant reminder of the course's location, even
when the beautiful vistas of the ocean are hidden.

While Paraparaumu Beach Golf Club was in existence prior to the
Second World War, it was not until 1946 that it became the course it
is today. At that time, two prominent New Zealand golfers, Douglas
Whyte and Alex Russell, decided to take the existing layout and trans-
form it into something that befitted its gorgeous location.

Whyte, an excellent amateur golfer, and Russell, an architect who
had assisted Alister Mackenzie with his work at Royal Melbourne,
went to work on laying out a course with a touch of Scotland in it.
Economy is a fair word to describe how the course was built. Nothing has been done in extreme.

The new Paraparaumu Beach Golf Club was crammed into 130
acres, not a lot of land for eighteen championship holes. Despite this,
however, the course has a sense of being wide open. There is a feel

*The Scottish
influences are
everywhere at
Paraparaumu
Beach.*

*The beauty of the New Zealand countryside
is unparalleled.*

133

Paraparaumu Beach, ctd.

Paraparaumu Beach Golf Club was redesigned after the Second World War by Douglas Whyte and Alex Russell.

of space and freedom, which can be attributed to its design.

A round at Paraparaumu Beach requires great thought. Off the tee, placement must be contemplated well in advance. Hitting straight down the middle is not always the best idea. The bunkers are infrequent here, but each one is in play. Rising and falling fairways often hide the sandy hazards for the first-time player such as on the 3rd hole, where a bunker lies waiting to catch balls. It, like many other bunkers on the course, play an integral part of decisions on course management.

Once into the fairway, more careful consideration must be given to the approach shots into the greens. They are undulating and filled with swales and can cause grief to all but the best of putters.

Like all courses situated near open water, the wind is a large factor at Paraparaumu Beach Golf Club. It can often switch directions from day to day, bringing a variety of intensities along with it. During one national amateur championship, a player choked down on a nine iron on one day to record a hole-in-one on the 14th. The very next day, he came to the same hole and hit a three iron that just reached the green.

The greens at Paraparaumu Beach are subtly deceiving, and great care must be taken when lining up a putt.

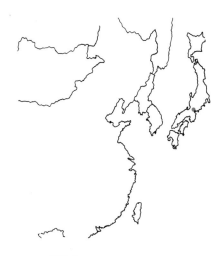

Shinyo

Nagoya, Japan

Shinyo seems to fit into the surrounding terrain. Holes such as the 13th, despite its unusual bunker patterns, flow easily.

Anyone familiar with the design work of Desmond Muirhead would certainly not call it conservative. The radical, off-beat course architect who once commented that he had very little allegiance to St. Andrews has constructed some of the most unusual courses in the world. Coincidentally, they are also some of the best.

In Japan, Muirhead is known for the Shinyo (New Sun) Country Club, a magnificent and graceful golf course. Shinyo is owned by Nitto Kogyo, a large company that owns more than thirty courses in Japan as well as the Turnberry Hotel and Golf Courses in Scotland. It commissioned Muirhead to tackle the job of building a course an hour from Nagoya. When Muirhead first set eyes upon the land, he was disappointed. It offered very little, just a vast, uninteresting patch near some mountains. His mood changed, however, and he took on the task of crafting Shinyo.

What has resulted is a course that, unlike many others in Japan, seems to fit naturally into the

The 7th hole features a fan-shaped grass hazard in front of the island green.

countryside. While there are certainly many contrived portions of the course, as befits a Muirhead design, everything seems calm and smooth. The hard edges are accepted.

The beauty of the nearby mountains seems fitting for this course, which has many rising and falling fairways. From most points of the course, the snowcaps can be seen and often are used as reference points or targets for shots.

One of the much-anticipated Muirhead touches at Shinyo comes at the 7th hole, a par three with a green set into a pond. At the front of the green sits a portion of grass shaped like a Japanese fan complete with undulations. Its existence seems almost ridiculous, but it serves as a very good hazard.

On the 12th hole, players will find a series of traps from which they may never be able to extricate themselves. A lake with waterfalls also comes up the hole and splits the green in two. It is a hole that may stun people with its design but tempt them to make a par.

Building a course in Japan is never a cheap affair, and Shinyo was no exception. A bridge on the course—which spans a 40-foot gully—was said to have cost $1 million. But with memberships selling at more than $425,000, the expense seem worth it.

Shinyo is certainly a memorable course. It is unlikely that many of the holes, with their Muirhead influences, will ever be forgotten.

Titirangi *New Lynn, Auckland, New Zealand*

The Titirangi Golf Club first came in to being in 1915, when land in New Lynn was cleared and seeded. Over the next few years, the course became more and more viable although little golf was played due to the First World War.

By 1918, the club, originally known as the Maungakiekie Golf Club, was finished. In 1920, a clubhouse was built to accommodate the burgeoning membership.

While these events mark the official beginning of the Titirangi Golf Club, it was the redesign of the course in 1927 by architect Alister Mackenzie that brought it into prominence. Mackenzie turned the average course into one of high standards. His work has been left virtually intact since that time.

The testing layout has made Titirangi a popular tournament site over the years.

Titirangi has been site to many tournaments, such as the 1933, 1951, and 1962 New Zealand Opens. As well, the Air New Zealand Shell Open has been contested over the Titirangi course on twelve occasions.

Overall, Titirangi, is a finely crafted course. It offers great variety and challenge. The majority of holes feature gently rolling terrain and fairways with suitable landing areas. The greens are well proportioned, so the shorter holes have smaller putting surfaces, while those requiring a long iron or wood for the second shot are larger and more receptive.

Titirangi begins in a calm fashion, with two relatively short par fours of just over 300 yards, before it shows its teeth. The 400-yard, par-four 3rd hole and 500-yard, par-five 5th offer just a taste of what's to come. Some exceptional par threes, such as the 200-yard 14th, are also a strength of the course.

At 6,311 yards, Titirangi is long enough, considering it plays to a par of seventy. Distance and placement off the tee are necessities for a good round.

From humble beginnings, Titirangi has become one of the best clubs in New Zealand and continues to improve each year.

The unique style of Alister Mackenzie, architect of such courses as Augusta National and Royal Melbourne, is evident throughout Titirangi, including here on the 11th hole.

The green on the 2nd hole is typical of those found at Titirangi. Most are well proportioned in relation to the iron, which must be used for the approach.

Wairakei

Taupo, New Zealand

The Wairakei Golf Course rests in the heart of New Zealand's magnificently strange geothermal area, near the midway point of the North Island. Unlike most other courses in New Zealand, Wairakei was built to provide a championship test for Kiwi golfers. Until its opening, it was felt there was a dearth of courses in this country that could adequately host significant championships.

Wairakei was designed by British native Major John Harris for the Tourist Hotel Corporation, which hoped to utilize the course as a drawing card for the hotel at that site. The Harris design has a straightforward approach, with only a few gimmicks to spice up a round. Not much earth was moved in creating Wairakei, and the natural terrain has been well utilized.

The 1st hole is characterized by a large bunker and tree resting in the middle of the fairway. The hazard seems to attract golf balls the way a magnet draws iron filings. Another signature hole is the 14th, a lengthy par five of 608 yards. Impressive bunkering punctuates the fairway requiring precision in both the first and second shots. With those completed, all that remains is an iron to an elevated green shaped like a horseshoe. Pin placements can make this approach almost diabolical, and hitting the wrong side of the green could leave players with no way to reach the hole.

From almost every point on the golf course, the rising steam from nearby bore holes is evident. Clouds of vapors caused by underground geothermal activity rise slowly above the pine trees and seem to hang in the air. It's an unusual sight that will certainly intrigue visitors.

In 1990, the Tourist Hotel Corporation sold Wairakei to New Zealand Golf Systems. The new owners have spent a great deal of time and money to improve the course, adding such features as an irrigation system and clubhouse.

The elevated green on Wairakei's 10th hole is guarded by a pond on the right and a series of bunkers.

The 18th is a strong but fair finishing hole that has provided exciting moments for professional and amateur players alike.

CONTACT INFORMATION

Call or write the following courses for specific information. (Contact information was correct at time of compilation; the publishers are not responsible for subsequent changes.)

THE AMERICAS AND CARIBBEAN

CANADA

BANFF SPRINGS GOLF CLUB
P.O. Box 960, Banff, Alberta T0L 0C0; (403) 762-2211

GLEN ABBEY GOLF COURSE
1333 Dorval Drive, Oakville, Ontario L6J 4Z3; (416) 844-1800

JASPER PARK LODGE
Box 40, Jasper, Alberta T0E 1E0; (403) 852-3581

KANANASKIS COUNTRY GOLF COURSE
Box 1710, Kananaskis Village, Alberta T0L 2H0; (403) 591-7070

THE NATIONAL GOLF CLUB
134 Clubhouse Road, Woodbridge, Ontario L4L 2WL; (416) 798-4900

UNITED STATES

AUGUSTA NATIONAL GOLF CLUB
Augusta, GA 30913; (404) 738-7761

BALTUSROL GOLF CLUB
P.O. Box 9, Springfield, NJ 07081; (201) 376-1900

COLONIAL COUNTRY CLUB
3735 Country Club Circle, Fort Worth, TX 76109; (817) 927-4200

CYPRESS POINT CLUB
P.O. Box 466, Pebble Beach, CA 93953; (408) 624-6444

DORAL COUNTRY CLUB
4400 Northwest 87th Ave., Miami, FL 33178; (305) 592-2000

FIRESTONE COUNTRY CLUB
Akron, OH 44319; (216) 644-8441

HARBOUR TOWN GOLF LINKS
11 Lighthouse Lane, Hilton Head Island, SC 29928; (803) 671-2446

KIAWAH ISLAND
P.O. Box 2941201, Kiawah Island, SC 29412; (803) 768-2529

MERION GOLF CLUB ARDMORE AVENUE
Ardmore, PA 19003; (215) 642-5600

MUIRFIELD VILLAGE GOLF COURSE
5750 Memorial Drive, Dublin, OH 43017; (614) 889-6700

OAK HILL GOLF CLUB
P.O. Box 10397, Rochester, NY 14610; (716) 586-1660

OAKLAND HILLS COUNTRY CLUB
3951 West Maple Road, Birmingham, MI 48009; (313) 644-2500

OAKMONT COUNTRY CLUB
Holton Road, Oakmont, PA 15139; (412) 828-8000

OAK TREE GOLF CLUB
1515 West Oaktree Drive, Edmond, OK 73083; (405) 348-2004

THE OLYMPIC CLUB
524 Post Street, San Francisco, CA 94102; (415) 587-4800

PEBBLE BEACH GOLF LINKS
P.O. Box 658, Pebble Beach, CA 93953; (408) 624-3811

PGA WEST
56-150 PGA Blvd., La Quinta, CA 92253; (619) 564-7429

PINEHURST NO. 2
Pinehurst Golf & Country Club, P.O. Box 4000, Pinehurst, NC 28374; (919) 295-6811

PINE VALLEY GOLF CLUB
Clementon, NJ 08021; (609) 783-3000

SHINNECOCK HILLS GOLF CLUB
Southampton, NY 11968; (516) 283-1310

SPYGLASS HILL GOLF CLUB
P.O. Box 658, Pebble Beach, CA 93953; (408) 625-8563

ROBERT TRENT JONES GOLF CLUB
7995 Baltusrol, Lake Manassas, VA 22005; (703) 754-0630

WINGED FOOT GOLF CLUB
Fenimore Road, Mamaroneck, NY 10543; (914) 698-8400

CARIBBEAN AND SOUTH AMERICA

CASA DE CAMPO
La Romana, Dominican Republic; (809) 523-3333

HYATT DORADO BEACH
Dorado, Puerto Rico 00646; (809) 796-8903

LAGUNITA COUNTRY CLUB
El Hatillo, Lagunita, Caracas, Venezuela; (2) 961-1401

MID OCEAN CLUB
Tucker's Town, Bermuda; (809) 293-0330

TRYALL GOLF AND BEACH CLUB
Sandy Bay P.O., Parish of Hanover, Jamaica, West Indies; (809) 952-5110

EUROPE AND THE BRITISH ISLES

BALLYBUNION GOLF CLUB
County Kerry, Republic of Ireland; (68) 27146

CARNOUSTIE GOLF CLUB
Links Parade, Carnoustie, Angus, Scotland; (241) 53789

GOLF CLUB CASTELCONTURBIA
Via Suno, 28010 Agrate Conturbia, Italy; (322) 832093

CLUB DE GOLF CHANTILLY
Vineuil Saint Firmin 60500, France; (33) 570443

ROYAL COUNTY DOWN GOLF CLUB
Newcastle, County Down, Northern Ireland; (3967) 23314

ROYAL DORNOCH GOLF CLUB
Golf Road, Dornoch, Sutherland 1V25 3LW, Scotland; (862) 810219

FALSTERBO GOLFKLUBB
Box 71, Falsterbo S-23011, Sweden; (46) 40475078

MUIRFIELD
(The Honourable Company of Edinburgh Golfers)
Muirfield, Gullane, East Lothian, EH31 2EG Scotland; (620) 842123

PORTMARNOCK GOLF CLUB
Portmarnock, County Down, Republic of Ireland; (1) 323082

QUINTA DE MARINHA GOLF AND COUTNRY CLUB
2750 Cascais, Portugal; (1) 4869881

ST. ANDREWS
c/o The Royal & Ancient Golf Club
St. Andrews, Fife KY16 9JD, Scotland; (334) 72112

CLUB DE GOLF SOTOGRANDE
Apartado, 14, Sotogrande (Cadiz), Spain; (56) 792750

SUNNINGDALE GOLF CLUB
Ascot, Berkshire SL5 9RR, England; (990) 21681

ROYAL TROON GOLF CLUB
Old Course, Craigend Road, Troon KA 106EP, Scotland; (292) 311555

TURNBERRY HOTEL AND GOLF COURSES
Ayrshire KA26 9LT, Scotland; (655) 31000

VILAMOURA GOLF CLUB
8125 Quarteira, Algarve, Portugal; (89) 313652

CLUB ZUR VAHR
BGM-Spitta-Allee 34, 2800 Bremen 41, Germany; (421) 230041

ASIA, AUSTRALASIA, AND SOUTH AFRICA

BALI HANDARA KOSAIDO COUNTRY CLUB
P.O. Box 324, Denpasar, Bali, Indonesia 0361-28866

DURBAN COUNTRY CLUB
Box 1504, Durban 4000, South Africa; (31) 238282

FUJIOKA COUNTRY CLUB
Nishinakayama, Fujioka-cho, Nishikamo-gun, Aichi Prefecture, 470-04 Japan; 0565-76-2331

ROYAL HONG KONG GOLF CLUB
P.O. Box No. 1, Shek Wu Hui Post Office, New Territories, Hong Kong; 6701211

ROYAL MELBOURNE GOLF CLUB
Cheltenham Road, Black Rock, Melbourne, Victoria 3193, Australia; (3) 5986755

NEW SOUTH WALES GOLF CLUB
P.O. Box 28, Matraville, NSW 2036, Australia; (2) 6614455

PARAPARAUMU BEACH GOLF CLUB
P.O. Box 1544, Paraparaumu Beach, New Zealand; (58) 84561

SHINYO COUNTRY CLUB
1378-3 Hosono, Tsurusato-cho, Toki-shi, Gifu-ken, 509-53, Japan; (81) 3 3403-0511

TITIRANGI GOLF CLUB
Links Road, New Lynn, Auckland 7, New Zealand; (9) 875749

WAIRAKEI GOLF COURSE
P.O. Box 377, Taupo, New Zealand; (74) 48152

PHOTO CREDITS

All photographs appearing in this book are copyrighted by their respective photographers and may not be used in any form or by any means without express permission from the copyright holder.

Acknowledgements

Special thanks to those representing the golf courses who assisted the publishers in the preparation of this book, and to the freelance photographers whose pictures help bring these courses to life, especially Chris Ayley, Joanne Dost, Faith Ecktermeyer, Jim Moriarty, Jim Morrison, Larry Petrillo, Tony Roberts, Phil Sheldon, Tony Smith. The publishers would also like to extend their special thanks to Robert Trent Jones, Sr. and Red Hoffman for their support with this project.